ON UNIVERSALS

FORDHAM UNIVERSITY PRESS NEW YORK 2020

COMMONALITIES
Timothy C. Campbell, series editor

ON UNIVERSALS

Constructing and Deconstructing Community

ÉTIENNE BALIBAR

Translated by Joshua David Jordan

This book was originally published in French as Étienne Balibar, *Des Universels: Essais et conférences*, Copyright © Éditions Galilée, 2016.

Ouvrage publié avec le concours du Ministère français chargé de la Culture–Centre National du Livre.

This work has been published with the assistance of the French Ministry of Culture–National Center for the Book.

Cet ouvrage a bénéficié du soutien des programmes d'aide à la publication de l'Institut français.

This work, published as part of a program of aid for publication, received support from the Institut Français.

Visit us online at www.fordhampress.com.

Library of Congress Control Number: 2020910277

Printed in the United States of America

22 21 20   5 4 3 2 1

First edition

CONTENTS

PREFACE: EQUIVOCITY
OF THE UNIVERSAL

The present work brings together a series of essays and lectures spanning a little more than the last fifteen years, although I envisioned each of them as a continuation of the same investigation. The time has come, it seems to me, not to provide them with a "conclusion," but to test their coherence and complementarity. To that end, I have adapted them into French (when they were written in English, in the various contexts mentioned below), standardized and sometimes supplemented them (in particular with essential references).

These texts aim to problematize our conception of the *universal* in order to help clarify discussions of the meaning and value of *universalism*. The latter notion, hotly contested today (some now speak of a "quarrel of universalism" just as some previously did of humanism), is never univocal; it must be *pluralized*, or rather *differentiated*, for two reasons that together form a dialectic whose end point cannot be established in advance. On the one hand, every *enunciation of the universal* (the "rights of man," for example) is situated within a geographical and historical framework (which one could call a civilization) that affects it in both its form and content. On the other hand, the enunciation of the universal serves less to unify human beings than to promote *conflict between and within them*. In other words, it unites only by dividing. The task remains, however, of bringing a sense of order to the equivocity of the universal, an equivocity that at once engenders the excesses of universalist discourses and helps us to articulate the claims informing them.

At the center of this book are two long essays that attempt to problematize in a new way the contradictions of the universal and, consequently, its dialectic. In the first, "Constructions and Deconstructions of the Universal," based on lectures I gave in the United States in 2005, I develop, guided mainly by Hegel and his legacy (up to Derrida), the notion of conflictual universality, moving from enunciation to domination and from the latter to the subjectivation of the bearers of the universal, who measure the existing community against the ideal of universality. In the second, adapted from my contribution to an international debate in the journal *Topoi* (2006) on the task of contemporary philosophy, I examine the articulation of the problem of *universality* with that of *university*, describing the three major strategies that modern philosophers (from Spinoza and Hegel to Wittgenstein, Quine, and Benjamin) have deployed to think *sub specie universitatis*: disjunction, totalization, and translation. The figure of hegemonic conflict, discussed in the first essays, is here brought into philosophical discourse by way of its emblematic institution, the university (which has defined philosophical practice for more than three centuries), while at the same time confronted with its alternatives and relativized in its speculative scope. Totalizing the thinkable is not the only way to universalize it.

These two central essays are framed by two "discussions" in which I address the positions and objections of contemporary authors who have defended, among other things, a position different from my own, but from whom I have nonetheless borrowed certain notions and questions that seem to me important—in particular, those of Alain Badiou, Judith Butler, and Joan Scott (although I also refer to the arguments of Barbara Cassin, Dipesh Chakrabarty, Françoise Duroux, Jean-François Lyotard, Giacomo Marramao, Jean-Claude Milner, Jean-Luc Nancy, Jacques Rancière, Gayatri Spivak, and Michael Walzer).

Finally, in an "après-coup" written especially for the present volume, I attempt to specify once again what to my mind constitutes the essentially paradoxical nature of the idea of universality both in its theoretical construction and in its practical applications. On the basis of the previous discussions, I delineate *three aporias* related to the "world," to the collective subject (the "we" and its "others"), and to the political community (the "city" or "citizenship"), which together give the *new quarrel of universals* its inextricably philosophical and political character. I attempt to connect these aporias with other themes that have come to the forefront of my philosophical work in recent years, in particular those of anthropological differences and the unequal translation of languages that "are spoken"/"speak to one other" ["*se parlent*" *entre elles*]. The notion of a *multiversum*, situated not prior to but *beyond unity* (and whose complex of translating practices between idioms provides, I and others believe, the most plausible model) can be aligned, at the level of individuals, with the figure of a *quasi-transcendental subject*, for whom the ontological question that at once constitutes it and condemns it to errancy is precisely that of the multiplicity of differences of the human.

Hence the book's title, which should be read as a question rather than a thesis. *On Universals*, because there are necessarily many, which themselves can be understood in more than one way; in other words, they divide (*pollakhos legomena*) in a series that never ends (*infinita infinitis modis*). And because we ourselves *are* "*universals*," each time singular in our—by definition, uneasy—relationship with the forms, institutions, discourses, and practices that situate us on the frontier of the communities from which we receive our words and our places.

ON UNIVERSALS

1

RACISM, SEXISM, UNIVERSALISM

A Reply to Joan Scott and Judith Butler

Several years ago, I published two texts in which I set forth propositions concerning the paradoxes and ambiguities of the notion of universalism.[1] Not, I should point out, in order to recommend that the notion be abandoned or morally or politically disqualified, but rather to examine its construction, transformation, and continual refoundation.

In the first of these texts,[2] I attempted to show that one cannot clearly demarcate the two apparently antithetical notions of racism and universalism (or declared antithetical in most "antiracist" discourses, whose common and quasi-official basis is ethical *humanism*). I showed that "universalism and racism are *determinate contraries*, which is why each of them affects the other from the inside." As such, an element of universality and anthropological universalism (a certain conception of the *human essence* or *human model*) is always at work in the constitution of modern racist discourses (which hierarchize human types or groups according to their differential relationship to that essence or model). Likewise, an element of discrimination and even of generic exclusion is always involved in the constitution of a general idea of the human that *identifies* human characteristics or fundamental values and in so doing invests them with a normative function.

In the second text,[3] I attempted to apply an analytical schema inspired by Lacan (the tripartition of the real, the imaginary, and the symbolic) to what seemed to me *the intrinsic equivocity* of the notion of the universal or universality. I examined in their opposition and interdependence what I called a "real universality" (not only the interaction between individuals and communities within the same "world" or the same "globalization," but also their assignment to unequal positions of "majority" and "minority" status within relations of domination); a "fictive universality" (the constitution of ethical norms through which, in every institutional community, the identity of subjects is socially recognized as well as internalized by the subjects themselves); and lastly, an "ideal" or "symbolic" universality (in which community affiliations are challenged, not in the name of some idea of humanity, but in virtue of a claim to equal freedom or emancipation made by classes struggling against various forms of domination). I then took up the example of feminism and what I called, following Françoise Duroux's use of terminology borrowed from Jean-Claude Milner, the "paradoxical class" of women in order to show how such a claim can at once be maintained by a particular group, or, more precisely, by a particular difference, and yet concern an entire society, for it tends to subvert, to reconstitute on different bases, the political relation itself (which, in modern societies, most often goes by the name of *citizenship*).[4]

Now, it turns out that these two sets of propositions have been used in ways that to a certain extent pit one against the other. Although they were already somewhat at variance (insofar as those propositions relating to racism tended to describe the *negative side* of universalism as a *historical positive*, whereas those relating to emancipatory and, specifically, feminist movements tended to conceptualize the infinite *negativity* that gives universalism its capacity for political subversion), both nonetheless aimed to problematize the relationship between the universal and the community (in German, *Allgemeinheit* and *Gemeinwesen*, which immediately highlights the proximity of the two notions) or between identity and difference. At the very least, some interpretations have favored only one set of propositions without drawing the same theoretical conclusions.

The contrasts have struck me as all the more interesting because they have arisen in particular in the work of feminist theorists engaged in reflection and action devoted to transforming citizenship and, through that transformation, the very institution of the political in contemporary democracies. I have thus felt it necessary to focus more seriously on the question of the construction of the universal. I have especially had to reexamine the link between a critique of particularism, communitarianism, and discrimination and the recognition of the value and anthropological implications of differences. It hasn't seemed sufficient merely to juxtapose a negative side and a positive side. These are some of the initial elements of the reexamination that I would like to present here, beginning with some brief remarks about the discussions to which I have just alluded.

In Judith Butler's "Sovereign Performatives," a 1995 essay from her collection *Excitable Speech: A Politics of the Performative*,[5] Butler refers to my essay "Racism as Universalism." She wonders whether the thesis I develop in it—namely, that racism is present at the core of "current [or dominant] notions" of universality—can be reconciled with a normative, political use of the universal that aims to legitimize state suppression of hate speech (racist and sexist discourses). Certain "radical" theorists, often legal experts, call for precisely this, employing a specific category of performativity that allows them to erase the distinction between *speech* that produces effects (racist and sexist insults, for example) and *acts* (notably, acts of violence and discrimination). Butler maintains that while the dominant institutional forms of universalism are themselves closely connected with racist and sexist representations, as I argued, one cannot assume a *consensus* about universalist values (like equality) in order to make the state responsible for eliminating the verbal violence that stigmatizes minorities. Rather, we must recognize a "vulnerability" that inexorably affects the relationship individuals have to a shared language over which they have no control and, at the same time, implement strategies that counter violent racist and sexist speech, strategies that lay the groundwork for extending universality to disqualified groups or behaviors and challenge universality's normative naturalization of differences.

Joan Scott, in the introduction to the French edition of her book on history and politics *Only Paradoxes to Offer*,[6] connects her own plea for a "pluriversalist universalism," the latter based on the history of modern feminism and the contradictions of the French model of citizenship, with my use of the notions of "paradoxical class" and ideal universality, which tend to *transform* the community as such instead of integrating this or that "minority" into the *given* community of citizens—especially when the minority in question comprises half of humanity:

The paradox that this book examines is that born from the coexistence within republican discourse of two contradictory universalisms: abstract individualism and sexual difference. Whatever the specificities of their demands may have been [. . .], feminists had to fight against exclusion and for universalism while appealing to women's difference—the very difference that led to their exclusion in the first place.[7]

But this is possible only if women, dissociating the idea of gender difference from that of women's "generic" particularity or essence, appear in their demand for parity with men as the true representatives of an ideal of liberty and equality that forms the basis of citizenship, an ideal that that same citizenship has historically been unable to fulfill.

These two readings do me a great honor, but they are unsettling as well. It surely wouldn't be right to overemphasize the opposition between them, since they largely converge in denouncing the collusion between discrimination and abstract or, if one prefers, "bourgeois" universalism. Yet they are undeniably pulling in opposite philosophical directions. They can do so because the texts to which they refer contain an undeniable ambivalence. The question is whether this ambivalence stems from my choice of words, thus betraying their inadequacy, or from the thing itself, thus betraying its complexity. Butler has me say that *universality cannot be established without excluding* and hence that it necessarily contradicts itself; Scott has me say that *every exclusion is open to the challenge* posed by those who turn that exclusion's own principles against it. Whereas Butler's point of view concerns the *subject* and the strategies of subjugation or resistance that intersect within the subject, Scott's point of view concerns the *citizen* (more specifically, the female citizen) and how its institution transcribes and perhaps even formulates "human rights." At the very least, this ambivalence calls for some clarification, for it confirms the idea that universalism cannot simply be grouped among instances of domination (as theorists of difference and the right to difference tend to do) or among instances of liberation (as theorists of equality and the progress of equality tend to do), but represents, as I have suggested, the "site of struggle" against structural domination and the violence to which it leads. But this ambivalence raises the problem of how to apply in practice a principle of *decision* that differentiates universalism or allows one to choose conjuncturally among its various uses. At the same time, it raises the philosophical question of whether the deconstruction of the apparent obviousness or simplicity of universalist discourses might not expose oppositions that are *more fundamental* or *more determinant* than those between universalism and particularism or universalism and discrimination. I am thinking in particular of the opposition between universality as "inclusion" or "integration" (which I have elsewhere called *extensive* universality) and universality as "nondiscrimination" (which I have termed *intensive* universality), between emancipatory *insurrection* (which may not necessarily be violent or limited, of course) and the legal *constitution* of rights, and, finally, between the objective egalitarian *norm* and subjective *singularity* or *exception*.[8] All these questions are part of an overarching examination of the relations between the institution, the community, and individual and collective identity, relations that, in my opinion, fall within the province of philosophical anthropology and must—for reasons I will briefly indicate in my conclusion—be accorded fundamental importance for philosophy, and especially political philosophy (although, as the reader probably already knows, I essentially make no distinction between political philosophy and philosophy as such).

Rather than set out to answer these questions, I will simply position them in the following order. First, I will return to a hypothesis that I advanced several years ago and that seems to me particularly imperiled by the interpretive ambiguities surrounding the idea of universality I have just evoked. I will then try to show why we should assign central importance to the *institution* when examining the paradoxical relationship between racist or sexist discrimination and universalist discourse. This analysis will then lead me to posit, on the specifically philosophical level, a concept of "anthropological difference" that should help to distinguish between several uses of the—inextricably metaphysical and political—notions of identity, human essence or nature, norms, and normativity. Finally, by way of concluding hypotheses, I will consider what constitutes the apparently ineluctable paradox underlying the relationship between the politics of emancipation (or as one could also say, with some caution, a "politics of human rights") and the political community. Quite an ambitious program, you might say, and yet I can only claim to provide a general outline.

RACISM AND SEXISM: A SINGLE "COMMUNITY"?

The hypotheses that I believed I could advance in previous work concerned the paradoxical relationship between racism and universalism in the modern era. Of course, many historians and analysts agree that racism in its different variants—whether biological racism, based on the myth of racial inequality and thus on a division of the human species into distinct "races," or cultural racism, based on the transformation of linguistic or religious traditions into inherited antagonisms, as in the case of antisemitism—is an essentially modern phenomenon. However, the most important thing for me was basically to distinguish a simple social and political *utilization* of universalism by a system of domination that appropriates universalism for itself in some "private" way (as we see notably in the history of European colonialization and, more generally, in the Eurocentrism or Western-centrism engendered by colonialization) from an *intrinsic* determination of universalism by racism, and vice versa.

In this regard, I showed that the representations of a racial or cultural hierarchy constitute a crucial part of the process whereby *nations* imagine their own "election"—that is, the mission with which they believe themselves invested to save, govern, or free the world from the evil overwhelming it. Moving in the other direction, I also showed, following Michèle Duchet and the theorists of the Frankfurt School, that the representation of human progress as advancing toward knowledge and democracy is inseparable from the identification of "values" (the values, for example, of individualism or rationality) according to which human groups are in turn hierarchized and virtually differentiated according to the greater or lesser capacity they demonstrate to adopt those values as their own.[9] In other words, I wondered if it would be possible to identify what comprises *the essence of man* or the *telos* (the "ends") of the human species without positing *types* of perfection or imperfection (the "superhuman," the "subhuman," civilized man, and the barbarian), without establishing external and especially internal "frontiers of the human." But above all I tried to identify the subjective roots of this essence without neglecting the objective historical conditions in which such an ideological formation comes to be crystalized (a formation that one could, with Immanuel Wallerstein, correlate with the capitalist world-economy and its specific "worldview"). I thought I could link these subjective roots to what I called a *desire for knowledge* inseparable from the "being-in-the-world" of individuals and collectivities, which leads them to imagine their own identity, or their own "place" within the multiplicity of the human species, in a fixed and *univocal* way—that is, through the classification and naturalization of differences. The function of this desire for knowledge led me to hypothesize that the "racist community," within which dominant groups (but perhaps also dominated groups) project their own identity or shared essence and from which, in imagination, they exclude others, is probably not fundamentally different from the "sexist community" (in particular, the "male" community or, more precisely, the community based on virile misogynous and homophobic values) and may even coincide with it in practice.[10] I based my hypothesis on the observation of the persistent sexual connotations of the racist imaginary and the persistent racist connotations of the sexist imaginary, on the complementarity of functions that racism and sexism fulfill in the development of nationalism and especially of nationalism's aggressive and militaristic forms, as well as, conversely, on the *positive* example that feminism provides of effective antiracist practice. The latter does not aim to *destroy the enemy*, following a model that the democratic "class struggle" has itself not fully repudiated, nor simply to *empower the dominated*, but rather to *decompose* and *recompose* the community, a process that involves transforming the community's "customs" and collective unconscious as well as its ways of thinking.

To my mind, presenting things in this manner has always had the advantage of demonstrating that racism and sexism are rooted in (essentially unconscious) processes of identification that constitute personality and that are at the same time inseparable from individuals' membership in a community (and from their "formation" for that community). As Freud showed in his 1921 book *Massenpsychologie und Ich-Analyse* (*Group Psychology and the Analysis of the Ego*), racism and sexism are thus representative of the same "cultural discontent." On the other hand, this line of argument also runs into considerable difficulties, which Judith Butler's analyses bring to light. For racist or sexist processes of domination (and the violence to which they lead) naturally tend to instrumentalize not only their respective prejudices (and thus to mutually reinforce one another) but also *the resistances those prejudices provoke*. There is a "racist" use of feminism just as there is a "sexist" use of antiracism, daily examples of which can be found in contemporary relations between the Euro-American West and the Islamic world. It is thus impossible to imagine— except in a kind of utopian communism of emancipatory struggles that is regularly contradicted in practice—any kind of convergence or fusion of antiracist and antisexist resistance movements, even if one assumes (as many do) that to a certain extent they share the "same" enemy.

But is the enemy really the "same"? There is some room for doubt. In reality, despite the overdetermination of racism by sexism and vice versa (evidenced in major historical and anthropological works, such as George Mosse's study of the Nazi example[11]), the relationship of the two ideological and "cultural" formations to the *institution* are profoundly different, if only because sexism is a mode of domination that tends to the *inclusion* (and even to the domestic confinement) of its victims, whereas racism *resists this inclusion* and tends to the *exclusion, segregation,* and *elimination* of its victims, at least in the social and political sphere. And, moreover, because the respective histories of racism and sexism reflect completely different temporalities.

THE INSTITUTION AND DISCRIMINATORY FUNCTION OF THE UNIVERSAL

For this reason, we must say a few words about the central role that the institution plays in the paradoxical association of universalist discourse and discriminatory practices. This also means that the notion of institution cannot assume an unequivocal meaning here. I would therefore like to emphasize, very briefly, three closely related points.

First, allow me to recall that the structures of racist and sexist behavior, in their historical and even transhistorical dimensions (their "longue durée," if you will) as well as in their daily lived dimension, are absolutely inseparable from the existence of institutions such as the family and the state (which have in any case been intimately and increasingly linked ever since the family was "nationalized" and integrated into state "social policies"). By taking institutions into account, we avoid the symmetrical dangers of psychologism (which views discrimination as reflecting a fear of the other and of the otherness inherent in intersubjective or interpersonal relations, and consequently as either curable or incurable through adjustments to morals or education, depending on one's philosophy) and sociologism (which sees discrimination as reflecting collective determinisms fundamentally external to the individuals' actions). The institution (I could also say *power* or, better still, from Foucault's perspective, *power relations*, but on the condition that we never forget that they are inscribed in the very materiality of institutions) constitutes the essential mediation between individuals and historical collectivities: It is what determines the development of their subjectivity, the mode of their "interpellation as subjects," as Althusser puts it, and, as a result, their behaviors of reciprocal inclusion and exclusion, recognition and discrimination. But above all the institution constitutes the *source*, or the point of crystallization, of discriminatory representations and behaviors. We see this in the glaring way that the institution of the nation reproduces what I have called "fictive ethnicity,"[12] whereby racial signifiers make it possible, at least in the imagination, to draw the frontier between nationals and nonnationals, between "true" and "false" or "illegitimate" nationals, but also, of course, in the way that the institution of the family normalizes sexual behavior, prescribing what is "normal," and repressing, stigmatizing, and persecuting what is "perverse," always according to an unequal assignment of roles between sexes or genders. At the same time, the institution is the *target* of racism and sexism. I just now mentioned Freud and cultural discontent, by which I concretely mean family and state discontent. With the rise of racism in Europe in recent years, a racism more or less directly related to the constitution of immigrant workers into the scapegoats of the crisis of the nation-form and to the socially destructive effects of globalization, it has become abundantly clear that "spontaneous" racism is always, in fact, a discourse implicitly addressed to the state, which is "called upon" to keep its tacit promise to "side with nationals" over foreigners, and in which the weakest individuals fear, simultaneously and contradictorily, the state's excess of power and its powerlessness, in short, the collapse of its sovereignty.[13]

These power or institutional effects are all the more decisive because we are dealing with *universalist* institutions or with powers whose function and responsibility are the *institution of the universal*. Not merely in the sense that I have called "extensive," which tends to include within its sphere of influence, or within the domain of obedience of a given power, the maximum number of individuals and, ideally, all of humankind (which one might call the imperialist dimension of institutions of power), but especially in the sense that I have called "intensive," which assigns to the institution of power (for example, the republican nation) and to its specific "authority" the function of *detaching* individuals from their traditional affiliations and subordinations, of abolishing or neutralizing structures of constraint or discrimination (by declaring, for example, that "all men are equal before the law," that "men are born and remain free and equal in rights," etc.). We can agree with Foucault that modernity gradually deprives *sovereignty* of its political and social privilege in favor of more institutional, less "exceptional," mechanisms of power—those of *discipline* and *governmentality*. It is more difficult to agree with him, if this is indeed his position, that modernity has diminished the institutional function of the universal belonging to power structures that are themselves "universalist." But how then are we to understand the contradiction wherein the removal of constraints and discrimination has led in one and the same movement to the emergence of new constraints and new forms of discrimination?

The only possible response, of course, is that the principle of these constraints-discriminations is no longer the same, that it is to a certain extent the inverse of the principle governing the old statutory powers and caste privileges. In other words, it represents the flip side of the *institution of equality* typical of universalist powers. As I have maintained on various occasions, when I have intentionally given this thesis as radical a form as possible—notably in discussing the at least apparent paradox underlying the founding revolutions of modernity, which have proclaimed the universality of human rights and yet excluded manual laborers, women, slaves or, more generally, colonized peoples from citizenship—the exclusions made on the basis of the principle of equality (or equal freedom) are to a certain extent much deeper, and much more deeply unconscious, than the exclusions that derive directly from a communitarian particularism or from a hierarchical conception of the human species dependent on a caste system. For the former exclusions can only be justified if, in one way or another, the *other*, the *excluded*, whether internal or external, is represented as a "nonperson," if the other is cut off from the human species or, more precisely, from what is supposed to constitute (and in the very process becomes) *the normative essence of the human* or the *final goal of the development of humanity* (for example, "rationality").[14] This obviously entails a process of extreme symbolic violence, one often closely bound up with extreme forms of physical violence, humiliation, desensitization, and extermination.

But here a considerable difficulty arises—at least for us Westerners (and I stress this point because I am speaking in Tokyo, where I have come, for among other reasons, to try to "decenter" somewhat my spontaneously Western-centrist point of view)—that terribly complicates both the analysis and the historical exposition. For, rather than a single model of the institution of the universal, we are dealing with at least two, each apparently originating in a different period (which isn't a straightforward question) and, most important, deriving from different principles. We have the model of *religious universalism*, that of religions explicitly called "universal," which for us Westerners means "monotheistic," and the model of *political* or, better, *juridico-political universalism*, which, applied by nation-states, in particular when they present themselves as republican and democratic, seeks to extend itself beyond the nation-state to international institutions. The exclusions that each model imposes are guided by different principles: Heresy, for example, is not cultural difference, even if the two intersect and overlap (which is clearly the case with antisemitism), and even if the transition from the first to the second may itself be represented as an *evolution of the universal*, as a modernization or secularization, as a "disenchantment of the world" (Weber) that would nonetheless retain certain forms of legitimation of authority and certain forms of individuals' "subjective" inclusion in the universal community (above all morality, especially family morality). Several years ago, I myself contended that the "crisis of the national form of the state" irreversibly began with globalization, whereas the "crisis of the religious institution of the community" was far from over or possibly only in its early stages—assuming that it might ever come to an end.[15] Recent history doesn't seem to have done anything to invalidate the diagnosis. But the problem with interpreting the concrete and contradictory combinations of liberation and discrimination on this basis (for example, in terms of the family, the inequality of the sexes, and sexual morality) is that we think we already pretty much know *what a state is*, precisely because this political form has in practice been "universalized" over the course of modern history. Today, every individual in the world deals with more or less well-established states. On the other hand, we do not really know *what a "religion" is in general*. We even have very good reasons to believe that the term is ambiguous, except, that is, within the Western imagination, which is grounded in the development of Judeo-Christian and Islamic monotheism followed by the more or less total "secularization" of Christianized and Islamized societies. Yet if religion is not an unambiguous term, neither is the term universalism. Is Buddhism (if there is *one* Buddhism) a "religion"? Furthermore, is it a *universal* religion (which is how we tend to imagine things in the West)? And what then is its exclusionary principle? Or are we to imagine, from the point of view of universalism, that the "religions" and religious development of the Far East *relativize* monotheism's claim to provide the model for religious universalism and the starting point for theologico-political evolution?[16]

I won't pretend to answer these questions here, but I will note, before turning to the next point, and in anticipation of a fuller development elsewhere, that they have repercussions on two other closely related issues essential to the analysis of the contradictions of universalism. The first concerns the notion and institution of *equality* or, better, the intrinsic relation, at once discernible and indiscernible, separable and inseparable, between *equality*, *identity*, and *homogeneity*. Let us note that in French (but what about in Japanese?) these three terms may, in certain contexts, be translated by the single German term *Gleichheit*, which is a remarkable indication of the *intrinsic* character, internal to universality itself, of the contradiction with which we are confronted, just as the proximity of the German terms *gemein*, *allgemein*, *Allgemeinheit*, *Gemeinwesen*, and *Gemeinschaft* ("common," "universal," "universality," "community") indicates that this contradiction is specifically linked to the fact that the universal is established and thus realized and acknowledged in history to the extent that it becomes the ideal and norm of the community (compare the late-Latin doublets *universitas* and *universalitas*). The condition of *equality* between individuals, and more profoundly between subjects recognized as having the rights of citizens, at least tends toward an *identity*, an "identical" and therefore universal way that individuals relate to themselves, that they consider themselves individually, for example, as (alone) responsible for their actions. Hence it is fundamentally a collective *homogeneity*. Now, even if, in terms of both meaning and political consequences, it is not practically equivalent to view this homogeneity as "racial" and "cultural" or as the result of individuals' submission to common "transcendental" values, the logical principle of the construction of identity is nonetheless the same and has the potential in every case to lead to the exclusion of an inhuman or subhuman remainder.

From this first issue a second, closely related question arises, which I would hesitate to call more speculative, because it seems instead to bring us closer to the concrete practice of politics or, at least, to what constitutes the historical engine of politics. Namely, the question of whether the contradictions of universality, the paradoxical coexistence of (secular or religious) universalist principles, and the oscillation of our conception of subjective identity between the two antithetical but nearly indistinguishable poles of equality and homogeneity or the "same" (which a Lacanian would probably describe as the symbolic aspect and the imaginary aspect of collective belonging), which I have tried to show are inseparable from the process of the institution of the universal, are simply the *effects* of the institution or must rather be ascribed to its very *conditions of possibility*, which we might call the *institutive process* (along the lines of the "constituent process" described by Antonio Negri)—that is, the formation process of communitarian institutions (and especially of politics), whatever they may be. The stakes of this question (which, it would be easy to show, has haunted every examination of the essence of the political since at least the beginning of the Enlightenment—in debates on voluntary servitude, the respective roles of contract and law, etc.) are obviously considerable. They have to do with how—for example, in our conception of the relationship between abstract universal "human rights" and the positive historical "rights of the citizen"—we articulate the *insurrectional* moment and the *constitutional* moment: in other words, the moment of the critique of all existing forms of domination and discrimination and the moment of power's emergence, its assignment of the roles, functions, and therefore of the subjective, individual, and collective identities that inscribe rights in the social field.[17]

If we believe that the contradictions of universality emerge only *after its institution*, which also means that to a certain extent its concept (or "idea") remains irreducible to the institution, we can imagine that a revision, revolution, or democratic innovation might somehow make it possible to control and correct these contradictory effects in advance, to institute a pure, radically egalitarian and nonexclusive universality or a power that denies or limits itself, that *holds itself in check*, a power that would be a "nonpower" (just as theorists of Marxist communism dreamed of a state that would be a "nonstate"). If, on the other hand, we believe (as I do), in a more "pessimistic" but not necessarily resigned way, that the contradictions originate in the institutive process itself, or in the *possibility of the institution* (without which, in fact, there is no historical humankind), then we are compelled to admit, not that the form of the contradictions of the universal or the degree of violence of their actualization are immutable, but that the very principle of their emergence is irreducible. In this sense, even beyond the state and religion or the institution of the family, which is controlled more or less thoroughly by the state and religions and is the leading indicator of their crisis, basic forms of discrimination like racism and sexism will not purely and simply disappear but will assume new forms that are likely to combine and conflict, and will therefore remain at the center of a fundamental struggle over the definition of emancipatory politics. This struggle may turn out to be all the more decisive and difficult as these progressive or regressive forms appear within the context of a *"real" advance of universality*, within the context of the effective universalization of universalist discourses (a characteristic aspect of what we call globalization, to which the structures of the market, trade, and communication already provide institutional support). It is this last hypothesis that, by way of conclusion, I would like to try to further develop on the philosophical level.

"HUMAN ESSENCE," "NORMALITY," AND "ANTHROPOLOGICAL DIFFERENCES"

A long philosophical tradition has already attempted to overcome the aporia we have just encountered: It situates the internal contradiction of the universal, or the fact that the universal can only be realized in the form of a discriminatory "identification" that contradicts its own principle, among the very *conditions of possibility of the institution*. This is Hegel's philosophy, on which we are now more than ever dependent. If I had the time, I would gladly discuss it at greater length. Suffice it here to say that the mainstay of Hegel's solution (which is developed in the *Phenomenology of Spirit* especially but whose resonance is found throughout his work) is to think of the contradiction as inherent in the *enunciation of the universal*, as either preceding the institution or already present within it (in a quasi-transcendental way). The desire to express the universal (and for Hegel, one cannot not want to express it, for it is the principle of historical progress itself and, in particular, of the historical progress of emancipation), the desire to give the universal a name or to formulate its principles and the rights and obligations that derive from it with regard to human relations (whether "love thy neighbor as thyself" or "all men are born free and equal in rights"), is inevitably, always already, to *particularize* the universal, even if one imagines that one has not yet assigned it any content but only expressed an empty form. There is no form without content, no neutral form (for example, revolutionary principles imply an individual's "self-ownership" or a "possessive individualism"—as Hegel said even before Marx). The universal thus tends to function as one *particularity against others* (which it suppresses or disqualifies), which in practice means as a moral, legal, or religious *norm* disguised as a mere statement of fact or as a way for humankind to define its own essence. I believe that Hegel's description of the effects of the utterance of the universal is exactly right, and that it has the particular merit of drawing our attention to the fact that the institution of the universal is necessarily also a process that takes place in language and within the constraints of a linguistic structure. Yet this explanation is inseparable from a second movement, which is much more ambiguous even if no less intimately linked to our problem. I am referring to the fact that Hegel doesn't really *suppress* the reference to *identity* as a pole of universal reference against which "differences," "particularities," and "singularities" are recognized, classified, and hierarchized according to whether or not they contribute to the reproduction of a form of community. Instead, he *displaces* it, he locates it elsewhere (an elsewhere that is to a certain extent the place of the Other, what Hegel calls Absolute Spirit, in which we can distinguish, if not exactly the movement of history, the principle of history's incompletion, of its infinite advance as well as its coherence or *meaning*).

This is another way of saying that Hegel, as Derrida argued (especially in his 1968 essay "The Ends of Man"[18]), is very much a radical critic of "theoretical humanism" and of the definitions of human essence on which it depends (for example, humanity as rationality, as consciousness, etc.), for theoretical humanism is quintessentially a (finite) figure of the *enunciation of the universal*. Yet this does not mean that Hegel isn't a metaphysician; on the contrary, the power of his critique of humanism and thus of his elucidation of the contradictions of religious, legal, moral, and political universalism—and, virtually, of medical or "biopolitical" universalism, etc.—stems from his discovery of a way to recreate metaphysics, and thus to reaffirm the primacy of identity, by turning it into a metaphysics of the self-identity of Spirit in its becoming: that is to say, in history, as it passes through and relativizes all the particular forms of contradiction of the universal. With regard to this aspect of the dialectic, however, we are today living in a "posthistorical" age, not because historicity has vanished but rather because the postulate or illusion of the univocity of historical progress has. This is why we are in a position to understand what Hegel in all his greatness was nonetheless unable to understand—namely, that the dialectic of the universal in history also functions as a norm, that its principle, like the metaphysics of essence or the metaphysics of the transcendental, is to produce its own internal exclusions, even if this simply means drawing an a priori frontier between barbarism and civilization or civilizations of the "past" and those of the "future."

This is why I would like to counter the Hegelian problematic with a different one, through which I will try to understand, at least in principle, that which inscribes the contradictions of the universal (and in particular those that result in the persistence and continual recurrence of racism and sexism) not only on the side of institutional effects but also on the side of the institution's conditions of possibility or, what I have hypothetically called, the institutive process. I would suggest that this problematic does not derive from the dialectic, at least in the Hegelian sense, but rather from what in France in the last century went by the name of structuralism—which is another way of saying that I am by no means claiming to be its inventor, even if in its present schematic form it might not be found in any of the authors who have called themselves structuralists or who have remained all the more reliant on structuralism the more they have attempted to demarcate themselves from its canonical iterations. The problematic is centered on the idea of *anthropological difference* and is therefore, by definition, part of an attempt to revive what was once called philosophical anthropology, which is necessarily very closely related to social, cultural, and psychoanalytic anthropology.[19]

The question before us broadly concerns the equivalence between the perspective of *human essence*—a perspective without which there would be no naturalization of the differences between individuals and between groups, no representation of these differences as *prescribing the paths to individual and collective identification*—and the perspective of the *norm*, which governs the formation of institutions and allows sovereign or disciplinary powers to *regulate* individual behavior and to classify individuals in order, in the last analysis, to control them or, better yet, to compel them to control themselves. I must say that in this regard I don't see any fundamental difference between a perspective of "normality" and one of "normativity," or rather I simply see two sides of the same structure, one objective and the other subjective.[20] At bottom, I think that the equivalence between essence and norm, the essentialization of social norms and the normative interpretation of the essential characteristics ascribed to human nature (such as the opposition between cultures that requires individuals to *choose* the one to which they belong, or the division of multiple forms of sexuality between masculine and feminine poles, between passive and active, etc.), reflects the same principle of *anthropological difference* effective within a multiplicity (but perhaps not an infinite number) of fields—that is, within a multiplicity of practices essential to the reproduction and institution of life: the principle of the difference between "cultures," between "sexes," between a worker's "manual" and "intellectual" faculties, between "health" and "illness," etc. Yet these terms are themselves always problematic, for at its core the idea of anthropological difference is precisely that the human being cannot escape being divided, split into opposite types or models of individuality, even though *the site of this split or opposition can never be settled once and for all*—except, that is, by institutions of a necessarily coercive or violent kind. The idea of a humanity that would maintain no distinction between masculine and feminine or health and illness is inconceivable or meaningless in view of our history, but the question of *what the difference consists of*, or the idea of fixing a criterion so that a *boundary* might be drawn, unequivocally demarcating the domain of men and the domain of women, the realm of health and the realm of illness, is just as meaningless. The difference must thus be "negotiated," at once established (which is the role or rather the condition of possibility of the institution) and continually circumvented, subverted, and displaced.

I will therefore venture to say that universalism, not only as a dominant structure but also as an insurrectional principle or an ideal and infinite demand for emancipation, shares *the same source* as racist and sexist discrimination. Or, rather—because this apparently metaphysical way of putting things is far from satisfactory—universalism and discrimination are produced in the same "place," *in close proximity to one another* and in constant tension. For they constitute an attempt to think the unthinkable or ungraspable of anthropological difference or, better put, *of anthropological differences*, which are mutually heterogeneous even if they always overlap, and above all to represent the application of these differences to the human species, social life, and individual experience. Anthropological differences provide the basis for every communitarian construction, including the construction of a community of rights, of equals, and of citizens under particular historical conditions, and yet, in their instability and elusiveness, they are also the mainspring of countervailing excesses: symbolic excess, which pushes us to look for emancipation *beyond* any instituted figure of the community, in a kind of "community without community" (Jean-Luc Nancy)[21] that has always been the ideal, the passion, and to an extent the illusion of heretics and revolutionaries; and imaginary excess, which pushes us to reinforce the community with the bulwark of identity and norms, even if this means excluding or even eliminating the otherness that—as the community's "eternal irony" (Hegel)—threatens it from within.

As you can tell, I would ultimately prefer not to choose between the positions I have thought it possible to identify in Judith Butler's and Joan Scott's work. This is because, to my mind, their antagonism (a relative antagonism, I hasten to add) seems to me to reflect the very conditions of politics.

2

CONSTRUCTIONS AND DECONSTRUCTIONS OF THE UNIVERSAL

Allow me to begin by explaining the title that was announced for my talk and how I plan on interpreting it.[1] I would like it to be perfectly clear that I am not going to present any doctrine or outline any theory of the universal or universalism. In this regard, I may disappoint your expectations. Instead, I am once again going to test hypotheses related to questions of the universal, and to put them to work. The questions are, by definition, *philosophical*; we might even wonder if they aren't *the* philosophical questions par excellence, since philosophy is, after all, the discipline that endeavors to *speak the universal,* or "to phrase" (as Lyotard would say) *in the modality of the universal (sub specie universitatis)*—a nuance to which I will return below. Despite the risk of losing myself in not only abstract but empty speculation, I would like to try to develop a line of inquiry that addresses the *aporias* inherent in different *instances of enunciation of the universal*— instances whose stakes are always political, moral, and social—in order to bring to light their shared if not invariable philosophical principle.

So, why the title "Constructions and Deconstructions of the Universal"? First of all, it is the vestige of a project in which I planned to play off two types of approaches favored by philosophers who share the belief that the universal (*if it exists*) is decidedly not a *given* (as fact or idea) but rather a *process.*[2] A process, furthermore, in which the "opposites" of the universal (the particular, the relative, the partial, etc.) are continuously affecting or contesting the universal in return. With one caveat: For certain philosophers (the most important of whom, to my mind, remains Hegel), the process at issue is a progressive *construction* of the universal that proceeds by the internalization of its opposites within the concept itself, opposites that are thereby transformed into mediations of its own development until, from the dialectic, a *concrete figure of the universal* emerges. For other philosophers, however, the process we are dealing with is doomed to lose control of its own idea or question in a dissemination without end. Whether or not Derrida invented the term *deconstruction*, he remains for me the key reference here, because he subjected to critical interpretation all the *antitheses of the universal*—that is, all the binary oppositions that seem intrinsic to its definition, starting with the "logical" opposition between the universal and the particular, and thus with the identification of the universal as that which *differs from the particular*, in order to challenge the effect of *symmetry* that leads to the appearance of their self-sufficiency and absolute validity. Out of this deconstruction, there thus gradually come into view all the figures of excess, of the remainder, of supplementarity, that undermine the symmetrical antitheses of the universal but also underlie its construction by the very fact of their being suppressed. These are the figures of what is *neither universal nor particular, neither natural nor cultural, neither masculine nor feminine, neither rational nor existential,* etc. Applying Hegelian thought to the idea of a construction of the universal, I planned to ask how the finite and the infinite, contingency and necessity, are organized within the universal, how one might interpret the universal in terms of a resolution of contradictions or in terms of a displacement of differences. I would then have explored the affinities with different "concrete" or "practical" figures of the dialectical process—like *progress, education,* and *revolution*—that have all been associated with the idea of *universalization* or with its realization over time, in history, the world, and life. Then, applying the idea or project of deconstruction to different texts (including those of Derrida himself), I would have attempted to address the difficulty that many of Derrida's readers confront: Every settled notion, every "essence" or "relation," is presented in his work as deconstructable *except deconstruction itself,* because deconstruction is neither an idea nor a method but a practice without rules. This would nonetheless have led to the unsettling consequence that typically universalist or universalizable ideals—like *justice, democracy, cosmopolitanism,* and *enlightenment*—or at the very least their *names,* must preserve a performative value, as if they constituted the "proper-improper" "determinate-indeterminate" names for everything that might *open* our historicity to the essentially unpredictable figures of its alterity and alteration to come.[3]

But, as anyone can see, proceeding in this way would have inevitably placed me under the absurd obligation of choosing between these two styles or approaches and, consequently, of transforming them into antithetical abstractions. It didn't take long for me to realize that a mechanistic structure of this kind would be just as unfaithful to the one philosopher as to the other, for if it has always been impossible to read Derrida in isolation from his intimate and conflictual relationship with Hegelianism, it is no less impossible today to read Hegel while leaving Derrida aside. To put things plainly: Hegel undoubtedly operates a *construction of the universal* (as absolute, as idea, as concrete or dialectical universality, as process or, as he says in his *Logic,* as "method"). Yet he never does so without simultaneously operating a *deconstruction*: at the "beginning," as the moment of a preliminary critique or "erasure" (of *being,* of the *subject,* of the *immediate*—the traditional foundations of philosophical universalism), and especially at the "end," when he discovers (and has us discover) that the *infinite,* the *absolute,* designates a subversion of representation, names *the nonrepresentable element* of experience or history, which prevents the world from closing up on itself or "totalizing" itself in the figure of something complete or accomplished.[4] This also means, if perhaps less obviously, that when Derrida deconstructs the universal as metaphysical essence, as the crossing-out of the aleatory or unpredictable, the "possibilization of the impossible," the *propriation* and *appropriation* of thought and life through names and institutions, etc., he is also always already *constructing* a certain universality—even if it is in the mode of *fiction,* of a hyperbolic supersession of particular institutions (as in his notion of "the university without condition"), of an internal negation (as in his famous formula of "the messianic without messianism" and, more generally, in all those propositions of the type "X without X" that he borrows from Blanchot), or of a double rejection ("neither human nor nonhuman").[5] All of these are indeed *enunciations of the universal*; at the very least, they surely do not encompass enunciations of its opposite, as has sometimes been claimed. It is clear that the Derridean idea of *différance* is not at all "relativist."

In short, although I have retained this vestige of my initial project, instead of moving abstractly from a moment of construction to a moment of deconstruction, I will try to put each one to work within the other. I will be making extensive use of notions and propositions from Hegel but as much as possible in a way that already involves their deconstruction. For I am convinced that one can apply to Hegel (and even to Hegel *in particular*) what Derrida says, for example, of Plato: From the moment that his philosophy was committed to writing as a *text*, from the moment that we consider it in the *process of its writing*, it remains open-ended; it can neither be brought to a close nor reduced to the totalizing figure of a system, however dominant that system has been from the very beginning, and however inevitable the effects of subjugation it has produced.[6]

Here is how I plan to articulate these questions:

(1) First, I will review the demonstration that Hegel provides in the *Phenomenology of Spirit*: The enunciation of the universal (and, as a consequence, its *inscription*, its *institution*, its historical *realization*) immediately entails its transformation into its opposite (the particular, the contingent) or the production of its negation. I am going to ask, however, whether this paradox, which one could say constitutes the quintessential statement of *Hegel's theorem* of the universal, has only a negative signification, whether it represents a disqualification of universalism in general. Perhaps the universal itself is nothing other than what is *expressed* in this specific, very particular modality.

(2) Second, I will turn to the implications of another terminology, that of *ideology*, generally associated with Marx. On one level, it restates exactly what Hegel already describes, and yet it does so in a different way: Rather than reducing the universal to the particular, it elevates the particular to the universal. *Marx's ideology* is nothing other than the language of the universal itself in that it *effaces* the particularity of *the interest*, the "parti pris," of the *situation* that it expresses. This is why articulating the universal means taking one's place "within" ideology, or rather discovering that that has been one's place all along. The concept of ideology also implies, however, that to a certain extent the language of the universal has *no outside*, for resistance to its "domination" (*Herrschaft*) manifests itself essentially in the form of *internal dissidence* or counter-interpellation. Accordingly, the category of

ideology (which, by the same token, loses any reductive connotation) merely describes the language of the universal; it also reveals that language's intrinsic ambiguity and makes it possible to expose its points of heresy.

(3) In conclusion, I will discuss one of the structures that connects the enunciation of the universal with the production (or manifestation) of *subjects*, who, it must be said, are not so much "universal subjects" as "subjects of the universal." This structure is indissociable from the fact that the universal constitutes *the ideal* against which the individual subject measures the value and accomplishments *of a community*, just as the individual subject makes use of that ideal to compare different communities and to see them as absolute or relative, necessary or contingent, and so on. This may in reality be *the preeminent structure* that subjectivizes the universal, and in which the internal conflicts of universality become manifest *for subjects*; it thus also bears the seeds of revolt and heresy within universality and reveals the fault lines within ideology.

You have probably noticed, however, a certain underlying reservation or caution in my presentation, which will require me to reexamine it in a critical way. The fact is that other philosophers have privileged a completely different structure of the universalization of the subject: namely, the structure of *equivalence*, which is intimately linked to institutions such as the market and judiciary—in short, everything that Hegel placed in the category of the "abstract" universal but that Marx, or "utilitarians" such as Spinoza or Hume, and even Deleuze in his way, considered an autonomous form of subjectivation of the universal. We may simply have to acknowledge that, if there is an ideal of the community that can be expressed *sub specie universitatis*, as well as an idea of universal solidarity, fraternity, or hospitality *beyond the community*, there is likewise an ideal of equivalence in reciprocity and exchange that is universalizable and, at the same time, an idea of equality or "commerce" (or "the gift") that *exceeds equivalence* and that therefore arises from a completely different genesis of the universal.

It is obviously not my intention to develop all these points in detail here. I thought that it would be worthwhile to list them beforehand in order to indicate the horizon within which I hope to put the category of the universal to work (or into play) with you today. I will now get to the matter at hand.

Let us begin with the *inscription of the universal*. We will stick closely to the extraordinary demonstration that Hegel reprises in every one of his works but that constitutes the central theme of his exposition in the *Phenomenology*, where it enables him to concatenate the figures of consciousness. The demonstration enters in twice, following two apparently distinct dialectical schemas: the first, concrete and historical, the second, structural and formal.

Concretely, Hegel describes certain "universalist" discourses that have appeared in (Western) history and shows that, by the very fact of their enunciation, with determined *content* and a determined *aim*—implying that through them the subject of knowledge or culture (which he calls "consciousness") seeks to reconcile his or her internal certainty and his or her criteria of subjective verification with "substantial" objective truth—*universality turns into its opposite*: Sooner or later, universality appears as a *particular* discourse that excludes others, whether consciously or unconsciously, and is excluded (resisted or threatened) by them in return. At the extreme, this means that there is not only something "false" in the discourse of the universal but something fraudulent or self-deceptive. Such is the case, for example, with "observing reason" (the term Hegel uses to describe the methodology of the natural sciences in the Classical Age, after the Galilean and Newtonian revolutions) or with the *politeia*, the "constitution-of-citizenship" of ancient Greece, which, he argues (in his interpretation of Sophocles' *Antigone*), excludes the "divine (chthonic) law" of fraternity and filial piety from its system of civic virtues.[7] But perhaps the most important example is the conflict between the discourse of (implicitly religious) faith and the discourse of autonomous reason ("Enlightenment"), a conflict that immediately precedes the emergence of the "moral view of the world."[8] The dialectic of faith and reason is the crux of modernity, and Hegel endeavors to explain that the two discourses, opposed with regard to the content of truth, each one accusing the other of deception, both presume to possess the same power to understand the purely intellectual world (*Einsicht*) and are built on their particular *share* of truth and falsehood. Hence they appear as mimetic realizations of the same idea of the universal. We are all familiar with his presentation of the dilemmas of modern thought; its contribution to the configuration of what we call "modernity" has proven decisive. It is based on the application of a logical principle that Hegel inherited from his predecessors (especially Spinoza): *Determinatio negatio est*—that is, to define the universal or to express its properties, to endow it with a language and a specific end, is ipso facto to show that it is not "universal" but only relative to a determinate conception of the world; in other words, that it constitutes a *particular* discourse.

But Hegel's arguments go beyond the reversal of a category into its opposite in the form of what today we would call a performative contradiction. The movement he describes implies the exercise of a force, or *violence*, such that the universal cannot retain the stability of a finite representation but must *seek out totality*, pursue the inclusion of all determinations from a certain "point of view," until, by doing so, it falls back into the absolutization of a *partial* concept (in both senses of the word "partial"). *The more a discourse is totalizing* (as the discourses of faith and reason indeed are), the more it exposes itself to the irruption of *opposition*, to negation and scission. This thesis is again magnificently illustrated by the discourse of Enlightenment, which for us makes it the archetype of universalism: The more it turns the universal into pure rational form (a form of "pure reason"), the more it relies in reality on anthropological postulates, on an image of man and the human that suppresses a whole unconscious portion of itself and, as a consequence, the more it relies on the presence of an *unsaid* within itself. Let us be clear, however, about the sense of the argument: Hegel is not telling us that discourses of the universal, when expressed, have "fallen" into the hell of the material world or into a field of empirical reality that has betrayed or deprived them of their original purity. Hegel is no (Neo)Platonist. Indeed, discourses of the universal *do not exist prior to their enunciation*; they coincide with it. Discourses of the universal are always already inscribed in a context that Hegel describes as that *of writing*, and he wouldn't be in a position to provide this kind of abstract narrative of their constitution and decomposition, rehearsing their specific historical movement, were he not treating them as texts within the universe and network of all texts. At precisely this point, we can return to what I have called a formal or structural exposition of the dialectic of the universal's enunciation, which, as dialectic, manifests the universal's reversibility.

The second dialectical schema appears at the outset of the *Phenomenology*, in the chapter on "sense certainty" (*sinnliche Gewissheit*). In fact, the latter has nothing to do with "sense" or with the "sensible" in any ordinary sense, but concerns what Émile Benveniste calls "the subjective appropriation of language" and "the formal apparatus of enunciation." In a series of texts clearly inspired by a reading of these same pages from Hegel, Benveniste focuses on the function of operators that allow a given subject to introduce her or himself into the universe of language or expression—such as personal pronouns (*I, you, we*), demonstratives (*this, that*), adverbs of time and place (*here, now*), and perhaps also propositional connectors like the negation.[9] These syntactical operators immediately raise the possibility of universalizing the particular and particularizing the universal, of subjectivizing the objective and objectivizing the subjective: *I am here now*, saying the truth *for you*, and this may be any truth at all, you may be anyone, I myself may be anyone. But also: Depending on who I am, on whether we are here or elsewhere, on whether we speak this language or another—all entirely contingent things—the truth that we utter will no longer be the same and may even no longer be true.

Let us pause here a moment to revisit our initial problem. A simple way to understand the meaning of Hegel's analyses and to shed light on their relevance to contemporary philosophical discussions would be to reformulate everything by making a distinction between, on the one hand, *the universal* or *universality as such*, a notion that seems destined to remain an inaccessible ideal, a "thing in itself" that we cannot know but can nonetheless imagine as a regulating ideal, and, on the other hand, different *universalisms*, which would express a demand for universality or an attempt to express and realize, or even to appropriate, the universal. For a number of reasons, I cannot outright dismiss such a possibility. The tension between the infinite and the finite, or between constituent power and constituted institutions, does indeed seem to reflect a duality inherent in enunciations of the universal or, at the very least, in some of them. Thus, in a politico-religious context, the American philosopher Michael Walzer suggests distinguishing between a transcendent, "missionizing" universalism and an "exemplary" universalism (which could also be called *immanent universality*), both of which he says can be found in the Bible. I, too, on various occasions, have resorted to a descriptive distinction between an "extensive" universality, which one could also call universalism, and an "intensive" universality, the best—and perhaps, in fact, the only—illustration of which is provided by the "proposition of equal liberty" between human beings, wherever they come together as a community, however large or small that community may be.[10] In both cases, we return to the idea of a tension opposing two different ways of considering the historical institution. This also highlights the fact that "universalisms," as Alain Badiou explains exceptionally well in his book on Saint Paul, have institutional *foundations*, by which they are oriented and from which they derive consequences (or, in Badiou's terminology, to which they remain "faithful").[11]

Following Hegel's central theme, I would like to relate this point to a situation that has marked a significant part of our contemporary history insofar as, during this time, we have experienced the dissolution of the frontiers within which universalist doctrines have built empires and protected their monopoly over the interpretation of the truth—namely, what I will call the experience of *the universality of the conflict between universals*. Hence the contemporary reality of *competing universalisms*, which sometimes lead to *wars to the death* between universalisms. The situation is most conspicuous in the political and theologico-political sphere: In the twentieth century, liberalism and communism both developed universalist discourses that not only had an extensive aspect, whereby they tended to eliminate their enemy in order to establish themselves as "the law of the world" and "the law of humankind," but also an intensive aspect, which tended at least in theory to establish the equal liberty and equal dignity of individuals and human groups through different systems of mediation (on one side, "property," on the other, "fraternity"). Today, the confrontation between secular and religious universalisms, which amazingly seems to have revived the conflict between faith and reason described by Hegel in his chapter on the *Aufklärung* (although following a completely different historical trajectory), demonstrates once again that the universal cannot be expressed in the form of a universalist discourse, with its foundations and aims, without being *appropriated* and, as a result, without becoming the means of an *appropriation of thought, language,* and *life* itself by the subjects that carry that discourse within themselves or make themselves its agents.

Let us note, however, the ambiguity of such a proposition: Everything described as appropriation could also be described as expropriation or, better still, to use the oxymoronic term coined by Derrida, as "exappropriation."[12] In this case, the same enunciative gesture that raises a given doctrine to the level of universality at the expense of its opposite (for example, liberalism over communism, the "rights of man" over the "right of God"), and that transforms that doctrine into a circumscribed "position," into a particular "opinion," into a "property" of a subject, is also what *exposes it* to the conditions and risks of the universal, what destroys its defenses against the claims to universality—in particular the claim positing unlimited applicability and translatability. To those who see here merely a kind of free-for-all of opinions and doctrines, all of them competing on a universal market to obtain a dominant position in terms of recognition or validity, I would say that they are missing the mark. The "market" is in effect only one of the material and institutional structures that nullify or relativize the frontiers between semantic universes or competing universalisms. The important thing is that every universalist discourse is always confronted with its antithesis, with its internal limits or exclusions, and ultimately with its repressed content. But another aspect of this system of reciprocal delimitations is still more paradoxical and compels us to abandon the overly simple—and metaphysical—distinction between the universal as such and universalism in the singular or plural. For, the fact is, as soon as a major conflict arises over the claims made by certain "truths" and certain "values" in the name of the universal—such as scientific knowledge or the imperative of moral responsibility, or, in the political realm, the values of freedom, equality, and justice—the difficulty has little to do with the competition between universalisms (such as that between liberalism and communism), which at bottom denotes the existence of some point in common (be it a point of heresy), in other words, an agreement concerning the disagreement itself and the stakes of that disagreement, and has everything to do with a fundamental *heterogeneity*. Once again, we encounter something very close to the Hegelian paradox of "sense certainty," which is much more radical than mere differences of opinion: Quite simply, there is *no common language*. Or, in Jean-François Lyotard's terms, the "phrases" (or phrasings) of the universal are not mutually presentable, not even in the context of open debate; instead they form a violent juxtaposition of incompatible meanings and claims, which Lyotard calls a "differend."[13] The Lyotardian *differend* is in many respects a reformulation of the Hegelian paradox of the contradiction inherent in the enunciation of the universal, but it accounts for and anticipates the *multiplicity* of enunciations themselves (whereas Hegel's initial formulation has a solipsist dimension, laying the groundwork for an "absolute knowledge" belonging to the same "self"—*Selbst*—but located as it were *beyond universality*).

I will now move to my second point, for which I will bring in the notion of *ideology*. Marxism, which has shaped the term's contemporary usage, does not separate ideology from domination (even if Marxism itself has hardly been able to assign an unequivocal meaning to ideology, as if the concept that "validates" its intervention into the philosophical field were at the same time the most unsettled of its terms, the mark of an irreducible aporia).[14] Or, rather, Marxism treats the phrase "dominant ideology" (*herrschende Ideologie*) as *a single notion*, wherein—in accordance with current German usage—*herrschend* must be understood both in an intensive way (that which exercises or imposes power, control, or sovereignty) and an extensive way (that which "prevails" everywhere, allowing no exceptions to remain). From this perspective, we can say that ideology constitutes *the very language of the universal*, which should make clear that, in the strongest sense, "there is nothing outside ideology"—nothing, more precisely, involving discourse and writing—thus *no other enunciation of truth except*, that is, the enunciation of its internal otherness (Derrida's "no outside-text" ["pas de hors-texte"][15]). The *others* of ideology are its internal dissidence, its reversals, all those enunciations that resist and subvert the "dominant" logic even if they still do not allow us to make the leap into an "outside" that would be free of illusions, an outside of pure reality and truth. To mark this closure, should I have used another term here, the term "metaphysics," for example, which Kant and Heidegger employ, the former to signify the idea of an illusion necessary for thought as such, the latter to describe the notion of an erasure or forgetting of being (which is itself the closing off of universality)? Perhaps. The only problem is that the contemporary scholarship that reprises Kant and Heidegger to signify the domination of the language of the universal is itself haunted by the Marxian and post-Marxian problematic of ideology.

The Marxian concept of dominant ideology clearly originates in the Hegelian arguments whose main points we have just reviewed. If the enunciation of the universal constitutes both an appropriation (of language by individual and collective consciousness) and an expropriation (following the famous metaphor of the "back of consciousness" to which, by definition, consciousness has no access), this means that truth and certainty, but also truth and belief (or *the attachment* to truth), are continuously trading places between two simultaneously inseparable and noncommunicating scenes. The mode in which they interact is that of the *return of the repressed*. Thus, whenever Marx and Marxists after him have gone beyond a *reductive* conception of ideology—as the "reflection" of reality or the "false consciousness" of subjects and their societies—they have merely transposed Hegel. The expression *conscientia sive ideologia* that I am thinking of here appears in Marx almost verbatim (from *The German Ideology* to his preface to the

Critique of Political Economy). But by the sheer fact of this change in terminology, something comes to be added: a different emphasis or, indeed, a new problem. For to express the universal—or any proposition in the modality of the universal—is an *appropriation of the universal* by a subject at a certain time and in certain place. To express the universal therefore means constituting an *interest*, making the universal the instrument or foundation of a *power* (which may be, and even is *primarily*, abstract and symbolic). Above all, practically speaking, it means linking the universal with *violence*, with its own specific violence, which eliminates or neutralizes differences and removes in advance every form of opposition and *dissensus* to its legitimacy, even if the universality is of a liberal or rational kind. While Marxists maintain the idea that the relationship of the universal to interests, power, and violence is an intrinsic one, which doesn't affect it *from the outside* or in a contingent way, they add the following question: How are we to think of this process not only in terms of meanings, interpretations, and translations, but also in terms of social forces and their development, and thus in terms of transformation and the obstacles to transformation?

As we know, the word that encapsulates the Marxist answer to the question is "class": *class* interests, *class* power, *class* violence. Now, as we can see straightaway, this formulation is *tautological* in its more general, which is also its more rigorous, form: A "class ideology" is nothing other than an "ideology" plain and simple, since ideology is merely the enunciation of the universal from a class perspective, a particular or "private" interest (and in this sense, a "class interest") expressed in the modality of the universal.[16] Similarly, as we saw earlier, it is tautological to speak of a "dominant ideology" because ideology is nothing other than the universalized or universal form of domination, in both senses in which Marx employs the term. It is the ideology that *extends everywhere*, "in all directions," controlling or constituting the entire field of experience, the perception of objects, and the representation of the world, thereby forming what Foucault (referring to and competing with certain Marxist formulations) would later call the *historical a priori* of a given age.[17] But it is also the ideology that requires *obedience*, that "transforms individuals into subjects," although undoubtedly always at the price of certain exceptions "that confirm the rule": resistances, revolts, revolutions, and more or less self-destructive deviances. So, to recapitulate: Not only is ideology, understood as dominant ideology, "universal" or expressed in the modality of universality, it *is* truly the language of universality, *the universal as language*—if truth be told, the only one accessible to us.

And yet I am well aware that this simple equation is full of formidable consequences. We can list at least some of them here, drawing inspiration from the best of the Marxist tradition (which has not always been part of its official versions), but with the proviso that, rather than uncovering the keys to a solution, registering the lineaments of a doctrine or theory for inclusion within the field of the social sciences, we are raising a series of philosophical questions that are by definition aporetic, destined perpetually to undermine whatever solutions we provide. I will mention two of these questions, whose apparent dissonance we shouldn't be too hasty to reconcile. The first arises from another of Marx's formulations, which reads like a quasi tautology: "The dominant ideology is always the ideology of the dominant class."[18] This is the Hegelian side of Marx, in as much as Hegel can be considered a theoretician of the domination manifest in state power and in its specific form of "universality." The second reveals a more problematic idea: namely, that the *dominant* ideology is always the one that enables the representation of the dominated class within the system of domination itself (and that also enables the latter to *present* itself within it); the dominant ideology is not, in the end, the ideology of the dominant class (the masters, aristocrats, or bourgeoisie), but rather that of the *dominated* class or the mass of people qua dominated. This is the side of Marx that approaches Nietzsche—the idea that dominant ideology is a "slave morality"—even if Marx ultimately takes the opposite position. Obviously, at issue in these alternatives is the very way in which we conceive of the "ideological class struggle," or more simply the "ideological struggle," and the strange variability that, after Marx, affects the notion of a "universal class," which at first glance appears to be a contradiction in terms.

What is the meaning of a dominant ideology that is "the ideology of the dominant class"? Certainly not that a particular class—the bourgeoisie, let us say—possessed of an equally particular, self-referential "ideology," such as the ethics ("Protestant" or not) of unlimited accumulation, having succeeded in supplanting other classes and in establishing a certain system of economic and social exploitation, also organizes things in such a way that its ideals, moral principles, conception of the world, and particular aesthetic tastes are adopted by all the other classes and, if need be, imposed on them by force or education, thus ensuring that its ideological domination reinforces its economic domination and vice versa. This instrumentalist view of how ideology works is one that many Marxists have been tempted to adopt (including Althusser, notably in certain arguments based on the notion of *reproduction* in his essay "Ideology and Ideological State Apparatuses"[19]); it is also a view into which some Marxists have fallen for political reasons. But it has little to do with a dialectical construction of the universal and still less with its deconstruction. What Marx's proposition really means is that the class that, under given conditions, perceives its interests to coincide in whole or in part with the historical universal (for example, the expansion of the market to the entire world, or human production as the only system of interdependent practices) is *also* the dominant class. We must understand that the dominant ideology, which is nothing other than the enunciation of the universal, "makes" the dominant class just as much as it is "made" by it. In other words, *a class that becomes dominant is a class whose domination is "universalized," which likewise means that it is recognized by the dominated themselves.* In *Capital*, Marx is careful to analyze this mechanism in terms of the convergence or even reciprocity between ideology (the universalist discourse of human rights) and a logic of the market based on what would later be called "possessive individualism" or the "law" of private property.[20] He obviously doesn't dispute that the discourse of human rights corresponds to the class interests of the bourgeoisie (although perhaps only in *certain circumstances* but not in others, or only in considering the "group interests" of the class and not the interests of a particular one of its factions in power). But he insists that this correspondence itself has a universalizing function, that which turns "human rights" into an expression of the universal. This of course doesn't mean that these rights dominate without violence; on the contrary, combined with the universalizing process of the market and the expansion of wage labor, the discourse of the rights of man is part of an economy of extreme violence and can thus contribute to its institutionalization.

But let us also consider the opposite hypothesis: that dominant ideology, promoting the reproduction of bourgeois class domination, can only, in the final analysis, be founded upon "the ideology of the dominated," just as, in feudal society, the dominant ideology had to be built upon the universalist discourse of religion that exalted the figure of the poor, the destitute, and, in fact, the bearers of values of redemption and justice in the image of Christ. One would think that we are dealing here with a "Marxist" variation on La

Boétie's *Discourse on Voluntary Servitude* except that in no way does this hypothesis point to any kind of political apathy on the part of the exploited or dominated classes; rather than placing them in the role of victims, it makes them the protagonists of resistance or potential revolt, without which the dominant themselves would have no hegemony to exercise. If the fundamental notions of the Declaration of the Rights of Man of 1789—liberty and equality or property and security—were only the functional conditions for the development of the market, they would have no power to engender obedience, no power, in the most general sense, to engender the *validity* of norms (as Max Weber would say). They have this power because they are *political* notions that bear the trace of emancipatory struggles and may one day bring about others. In short, they are not only "bourgeois" but *popular*, democratic, or "demotic" as well.[21]

Above all, this formulation tells us that in every dominant and therefore "universalist" ideology there necessarily resides a more or less active core of subaltern, dominated values. This holds true as much for monotheistic religions as for the discourse of natural rights, and we should probably examine still other examples, as well (I continue to think of Buddhism here). For subalterns do not necessarily remain passive. We should thus understand, following Foucault as well as one of the tendencies in Marx's work, that the struggle of the dominated expressed in the language of the universal is not only not incompatible with domination but in a sense constitutes its condition of possibility, since this struggle forces the dominant class to universalize its own language so that that language can "represent" collective social interests and not simply its own group interests in the narrow sense. Such is true, however, only on the additional condition that room be made for the *exception* and *excess*, precisely that which is not "representable" but belongs instead to the repression or even forfeiture of the universal. And with this comes the apparently inevitable consequence that the people of the dominated, the demos always already represented as a subject, subjugated to the universal, are simultaneously deprived of their own language, dispossessed of the possibility of *breaking discursively* with the dominant universality, and barred from challenging its injustice from within by "turning" the use of dominant values against domination. This also means that the demos seems in practice condemned to a choice between a resistance that *reproduces* domination and a pure violence that destroys it only in the imagination.

We are thus faced with an apparently insoluble dilemma. Unless, that is, there is indeed some narrow way out of the impasse, as certain of Marx's texts imply: those in which he, perhaps ironically, takes up the Hegelian expression "universal class" but gives it a subversive meaning compared to the one it has in the *Philosophy of Right* (1821), where it refers merely to the group of intellectuals and civil servants charged by the state with deliberating on "universal matters," on ideas or the *general intellect*. It is remarkable, in fact, that in Marx "universal class" refers in an essentially *equivocal* way *either* to the dominant class *or* to the dominated class. In other words, it designates, on the one hand, the class that "appropriates the universal" and constitutes itself by means of the construction of the universal as the dominant ideology, and, on the other, the class that is "expropriated," in the literal sense, from the means of production, from the product of labor, and simultaneously from universality itself, since universality is expressed *above all* as the recognition of the rights of the demos or the masses but is not expressed by these masses themselves, or at least not in the same terms and in the same way.[22] Strictly speaking, then, the notion of universal class *does not refer to a subject of discourse*, one that is "unique" (or "total"), but rather to the *unity of two antagonistic subjects*. Taken a step further, this could lead us to posit that it does not refer to a "subject" at all (the great quasi-transcendental illusion of those who have employed the notion of universal class after Marx[23]) but rather to a *scission of the universal*, to the irreducible dissonance of the "voices" that "speak" the universal—even in the extreme paradoxical form of a half-imposed, half-declared *silence*. At bottom, the notion points to an underlying fault line—in how the discourse of the universal is taken up by groups, classes, or parties and in how that discourse makes them its "subjects"—between, on one side, the production of consensus, compliance, and identification with the names of the universal and, thus, with the names of the majority's agreement on the values of a *community*, and, on the other, the production of what Jean-Claude Milner, in an obvious variation on the theme of "universal class," calls a "paradoxical class."[24] We could attempt to use the latter notion to reformulate the Marxist theory of "ideological class struggle," although it would hardly be an easy task. And yet it is interesting that feminists like Françoise Duroux in France and Joan Scott in the United States (albeit with some nuances and divergences between them) have effectively used the notion to put a name to women's nonidentity with themselves (or with their own "class"), in as much as nonidentity has been formulated by an emancipatory movement still profoundly divided on the question of "identity."[25] A class that is also a "nonclass" does not depend on the possibility of generalizing a given model of consciousness or praxis, but rather, *negatively*, on its members' rejection of the law of the dominant discourse (which Hegel, describing Antigone, calls "irony"). It depends, therefore, on a capacity to *suspend* the mechanisms of domination, which seems like a cunning way to circumvent the Hegelian paradox of enunciation without giving up universality or the right to speak. It also seems like a way of registering within the very definition of ideology the ambivalence of the two possible politico-philosophical interpretations of its relationship to domination.

I now come to the third point I mentioned at the start. It will serve as a provisional conclusion to my remarks. *Who are* the subjects of the universal? Or, if you prefer, what is the modality of subjectivation of the enunciation *sub specie universitatis*? You will have gathered that I have coined the expression on the model of the Spinozist formula (*aliquid*) *intelligere* (or *considerare*) *sub specie aeternitatis*, which we might translate as: to state propositions, to know things or individuals "under the aspect of the eternal"—that is, both from the point of view of their essence and their singularity.[26] The subjects with which we will be dealing here are those who "speak" the universal in order to affirm, challenge, or subvert it. But they are also those who are "spoken," expressed or, if you like, "called," "interpellated," as Althusser suggests, by and in the name of the universal. In order to be a subject *of universalizing enunciation* in this sense, it seems at first glance sufficient to be given a name within a symbolic genealogy, the title of citizen within a nation, to be baptized or circumcised, to have made and received a promise within the framework of a contract, and so on. In other words, the subjects of the universal are *institutional* subjects. This is why we are all always already individually and collectively subjects of the universal, which in return accords us the possibility of interpellating the universal or of calling it into question, but which never prescribes a single way of doing so. Inscription in the register of the universal opens a field of possibilities to which it simultaneously assigns certain limits.

In Louis Althusser's unfinished and now famous if still enigmatic essay "Ideology and Ideological State Apparatuses" (1970), written just after the events of May '68 to which, without having participated in them, he hypothetically applied the term "mass ideological revolt" (which we might translate as a mass revolt within and against the universal), Althusser merges two sets of structural observations.[27] Adapting the Freudian description of the unconscious to ideology, he calls ideological universality *eternal*—ideological because "ignoring the contradiction" (or denying it in its very movement)— and describes it as *self-evident*, in the sense both of something that goes without saying and of something that is immediately given with certainty— for example, the fact that we are "here," "now," and that we are "ourselves," which may mean anyone, at any time, and in any place mentioned in the enunciation. The echo with the Hegelian dialectic of "sense certainty" is manifest here and helps us to understand why Hegel's text might itself be read as a formal description of an *elementary ideological effect*, that which enables the subject to *find a place* within the universal (or to inhabit it), but also dooms the subject to oscillate continually between appropriation of the world and expropriation of the self in the name of the universal, to a perpetual exchange of irreducible singularity for absolute generality. Similarly, I think we should perceive Hegel's influence in Althusser's other indication, where he refers to the subject's *personal interpellation*, a subject summoned to submit to the law and, therefore, also inevitably impelled to transgression, to reaction and revolt. But this description implies that *the universal expresses itself*, that it "speaks" with the voice of an injunction or request, that it thus appears in the almost hallucinatory form of a double, an Other, or a Sovereign (subject). And here the reader of Hegel (and a fortiori of a Hegel deconstructed or deconstructing himself) might raise a few questions.

The Althusserian model of interpellation is explicitly drawn from the story of monotheistic religions: It comes from the Bible (Exodus 3), where Moses, before rallying his people around him to proclaim the Law, is himself called by Yahweh to Mount Horeb—the first link in a chain of repetitions that constitute "religion" or "revelation" as such. But this reference, as we know (and as many commentators of Althusser have troubled over), is always combined with another reference to the *legal status of the subject* as a "person," following in the tradition of natural law and bourgeois positive law. In both cases, a notion of *authority* is invoked, suggesting that the model of subjectivation in the ideological language of the universal "responds" to a command and obeys a law that transcends people and their empirical motivations (ordinarily called "subjective") specifically because of its universal character. Is this the only possibility? As I recalled when I began, Marx also described another model, one more directly associated with the practice of exchange and the structure of the market, and thus one more closely linked to the type of material universality that capitalism has historically imposed: the model of *equivalence*. From this perspective, subjects who are inscribed in the language of the universal (a "rational" "objective" language, a language of "utility," which is also a legal and moral value) do not appear as singular but as *interchangeable*—that is, they take their place within an indeterminate chain of exchanges and substitutions, just as commodities themselves are exchanged and substituted as equivalents.

Why did Althusser so steadfastly ignore this typically Marxist line of argument, which corresponds to what Marx called the "fetishism" of commodities and people (let us not forget that fetishism also applies to people)? The reason is clear although it warrants explanation: A subject interpellated by an authority that speaks in the name of the universal, or an individual who *imagines* being interpellated by such a law or authority (which is basically the mechanism Althusser describes), becomes ipso facto a member of the *community* governed by that law. In saying "I" and thus *being* "I" (for "to be" I is *to say I*, which is the very essence of the "first person"), the subject becomes "We" and *says* "We" implicitly (or "tacitly," the term classical social-contract theorists have such a penchant for). The subject says (that) We are "all of us together" this or that, sometimes in several ways at once, but sometimes in only one way, on the condition of sacrificing certain presumably particular (or, as we put it in the language of contemporary French politics, "communitarian") forms of belonging for other presumably "universal" (or, in Rousseauian parlance, "general"[28]) forms of belonging. And sometimes we attempt to *reverse* these definitions and this hierarchical order of belongings and communities expressed by "us" (or *all of us*): as when Antigone, in the Sophocles play interpreted by Hegel, cites "unwritten laws" to champion a community founded on love over one founded on war. Hegel, at the beginning of Chapter 4 of the *Phenomenology*, allegorically places in the mouth of Spirit (i.e., of the historical universal) the extraordinary phrase that expresses the essence of the politico-speculative operation at issue here: "*Ich, das Wir, und Wir, das Ich ist*" (I that is We, We that is I, or more precisely: We that I am, I that We are). It should now be easier to understand why, at the start of our discussion, although I recognized the need to analyze another, parallel structure of subjectivation—a structure founded on equivalence and equality—I proposed to complete the equation established between the concepts of universality and ideology with the idea that *the universal expresses the ideal of the community.* This is quite evident in the case of the State, Nation, Church, Revolutionary Parties, University, or "scientific community." Yet the proposition must be generalized to include every community, at least every community that doesn't present or perceive itself to be a mere *state of affairs* but instead claims to adhere to a value, principle, or ideal, even if the community can never *coincide* absolutely, with no remainder, with its ideal of universality. The latter, which we could also call its *transcendental double*, must always represent a *supplement* or *excess* with respect to the empirical, institutional construction of the community. But it is an internal supplement, an indispensable part of the construction itself. *Constituting communities, expressing the universal, or developing a dominant ideology within which individuals assemble to "reconcile" their divergent interests and incompatible convictions—these are all in fact the same thing.*

Obviously, the internal supplement or excess of universality can appear in different guises, which aren't equivalent from an ethical or political point of view. It is not the same thing to construct an ideal of community or a model of universality based on racial or ethnic purity and the linguistic or cultural specificity of the nation and one based on "fundamental rights," the republican legal system, fraternity, hospitality, and cosmopolitanism or internationalism. Some years ago, I risked entitling an essay "Racism as Universalism," which I concluded with a call to deconstruct those ideas of community that are founded on the representation of race and gender as universal characteristics of humankind, raising the possibility of a "conflict of interpretations" within the discourse of the universal itself—since the universal has no outside.[29] In a similar vein, we can complement the meaning of *conflictual universality*, a term borrowed from Judith Butler, to illustrate and develop the Hegelian concept of a universal that paradoxically turns its enunciation against itself or contradicts itself performatively. In view of certain recent events, at a time when the universal is expressed in the missionizing mode in order to expand the hegemony of certain values (like *democracy*)—which certainly represents one of the most *violent* modes of "forcing" a resolution on conflicts within the universal—I am tempted to add that the most effective deconstruction of domination is precisely the one that *intensifies the paradox*, that never ceases to return discourse to the *differend*, demonstrating, in this way, that every unity imposed by authority is a fiction and every consensus another name for contradiction.

SECOND LECTURE

When Carol Murphy, the director of the France-Florida Institute, came to see me in Paris to invite me to speak with you today, I warned her that my work may not do much to clarify the overarching theme of this year's colloquium—namely, the relationship between language, the visual, and "new virtual realities."[1] She told me that what they were hoping for instead was that I present my current work as it relates to general questions of critical theory. So, that is what I am going to do, with the caveat that my aim will be simply to build connections between previous arguments and interpretations and those arguments and interpretations still to come. I would like to take advantage of the opportunity you have given me to work through certain propositions whose conclusions remain elusive to me, in the hope of bringing the words to say something a little bit different from what they say traditionally, even as I draw on terms that we all know and use every day.

These hypothetical propositions have to do with what I call the enunciation of the universal, or better *the enunciation in the modality of the universal*, an expression I have coined in the light of other formulas with which we are already familiar: that of Spinoza, who speaks of knowing things "under the aspect of eternity" (*sub specie aeternitatis*), and that of Foucault, who speaks of the philosophical and political question posed by the act of "truth-telling," which the Greeks, under the term *parrhēsia*, made one of the bases of what today we call democracy.[2] The fact of "speaking the universal," with all the difficulties that it entails, does not, however, coincide with either of these two models, even if it inevitably overlaps with both. Rather, it poses specific problems of construction and deconstruction, a few of which I would like to try to set out and address here, without making any claim to exhaustivity.

There are certainly numerous ways of approaching the question of the enunciation of the universal, and in particular the question of knowing what distinguishes it from the metaphysical operation of *defining the universal* and establishing its criteria. Indeed, it would be tempting to compare the two approaches, associating each with specific objects, circumstances, and above all texts, whose differences one would endeavor to bring to light. For there are criteria of universality, just as there are criteria of truth—at least this is what a substantial portion of the philosophical tradition has believed. Let us recall, for example, Rousseau's formulation in *The Social Contract* regarding the law and the *General Will*, the latter of which he thereby turned into what would later become one of most successful and most effective *names of the universal*:

> I have already said that the general will cannot relate to a particular object [for example—and please excuse my use of current events to illustrate Rousseau's point—students wearing an Islamic veil in school or a seriously ill, comatose patient on life support]. [. . .] But when the whole people makes a ruling for the whole people it is concerned with itself alone, and the relationship, if created, is between the whole object from one point of view and the whole object from another, the whole remaining undivided. Then the matter on which the ruling is made is general, as is the will that makes it. It is this act that I call a law. [. . .] We can see also, since the law combines universality in its object with universality of will, that anything ordained by a man on his own account, whatever his position, is not a law. Even what the sovereign ordains concerning a particular object is not a law, but a decree; nor is it an act of sovereignty, but of administration.[3]

Forgive me this long quotation from a great author—who passes for so exceedingly French and yet was not—for it indeed has some bearing on the matter at hand. Clearly, one can consider the question of the enunciation of the universal, in what distinguishes it from the question of definition or criteria, either from a constructivist or from a deconstructivist point of view. This is what I initially thought of doing, and I leave it to you to imagine the names that first came to mind to illustrate each of these perspectives. But I abandoned that approach because it seemed to me that, perhaps even after devoting a great deal of time to the project, the essential task would still remain to be done: the task, not of attempting a synthesis, but of showing that the importance of a construction—and especially of a dialectical construction—of universality lies in the moments of internal deconstruction that that construction entails; that the value and perhaps the difficulty of undertaking the deconstruction of the universal, or of the oppositions it contains, lie in the possibilities of construction that that undertaking preserves or may even create anew. I therefore decided that it was better to bring the two movements together from the very beginning, to wrap one within the other, by examining what specifically accounts for the irremediably aporetic nature of the discourse that is expressed and that we express in the modality of the universal. It is a discourse whose disappointments we have a long experience with, but one that has lost none of its necessity, since in certain fundamental domains—in particular, the political—we are always already inhabiting it and are, as a consequence, unable to prevent it from defining the constraints on how we communicate.

This question, as we know, is a preeminently philosophical one, perhaps the very question of philosophy itself, which has almost always been presented as *a discourse in the modality of the universal*: a discourse of truth, a discourse of totality, a cosmopolitical discourse, a discourse of humanity and the human, and also therefore of that which exceeds and relativizes the human—the exceptions, as they say, "confirming the rule." But it is also a *political question*, and politically pressing, exemplified by the fact that the abstract, technical category of "the universal" has now, perhaps for the first time, entered the language of common debate, if not everyday language. Something akin to a "universalist party," or a party "of universalists," has come close to forming only to immediately fall victim to numerous divisions. To illustrate the question's ubiquity and urgency, it should suffice to mention a series of oppositions to be constructed and deconstructed, many of which in fact correlate with one another. For example, the oppositions between republicanism and multiculturalism; divine mission (or election) and tolerance and secularism; sovereignty, international law, and the politics of human rights; nationalism and cosmopolitanism (or internationalism); the market and culture as well as economics and ecology; or the opposition between "two cultures," one called literary, the other scientific; the opposition between philology and digital communication or translation and hypertext; but also the oppositions between liberalism and socialism, the class struggle and the race struggle, or the "clash of civilizations," etc. I have no intention of discussing all of these in detail, despite the interest they elicit, the stakes they involve, and the urgency there often is to clarify their terms. But I would like for us to keep them in mind as I venture to move the discussion to a more abstract level, where we will be dealing instead with the categories of *consciousness*, *ideology*, and *community*. Before doing so, however, I would like to make two remarks.

The first is that, while many of the antitheses to which I referred in this whirlwind review of the "commonplaces" of contemporary politics and ideology traditionally oppose the universal, or one of its names (such as republic or communication), with what seems to be its opposite—the particular, say, or the prioritizing of the particular (for example, multiculturalism or the race struggle, etc.)—many of these oppositions can in fact be reversed, can function *in the opposition direction*, and above all many, perhaps the majority, of them in reality put *the names of the universal* in opposition with each other. This can be interpreted as the sign and expression of a conflict between competing universalisms, a problem to which I will return in a moment. A good example is the opposition between liberalism and socialism, or between economics and ecology. We might even say that at the current juncture—leaving aside the question of whether it is actually something new—*oppositions of the type universal-particular are much less significant and intense than oppositions within the universal*, between its designations, determinations, and realizations, or quite simply between its rival enunciations, when the latter aren't merely serving to mask the former. The corollary of this phenomenon may ultimately be that *in the field of politics and ideology the particular does not exist* or *cannot be stated as such* without immediately transforming into its opposite. Indeed, as soon as one articulates a critique of universalism—whether religious or secular, political or scientific—in terms meant to defend cultures, idioms, or beliefs and their absolute right to particularity, *the enunciation is immediately expressed in the modality of the universal*—that is, expressed at once in a rigorously interchangeable rhetoric and from the perspective of a totalization and justification of *differences* as such, and thus from the perspective of another universalism.

My second remark has to do with the unique situation in which we presently find ourselves. Its uniqueness is easily verifiable, but in reality what I have in mind is *a problem*. I am thinking of the fact that the world in which we live and that is presented to us as the site of processes of transnational communication, as the immediate condition of our material existence (in terms of food, energy resources, and employment opportunities, for example), as that which is at stake in the alternative policies of sovereignty and law, of war and peace, of growth and development, among which we as citizens must choose—a world for which the prevailing term is "globalization"—is a world in which *the universal is not something to be realized but is always already realized and already present* practically and institutionally. Consequently, the enunciation of the universal, or, to revise Hegel's grand metaphor, the flight of Minerva's owl, does not occur at nightfall but at daybreak, for the cycle of universal history that is supposed to produce the conditions of that flight, to make the world and with it humanity definitively contemporary, eternally co-present, with themselves, has come to an end, and the performative or optative moods are now profoundly overdetermined by the constative. To a certain extent, in such a world *the universal is always already said*; it has nothing virtual about it and cannot be suppressed. On the other hand, everything that once presented itself historically as universalism due to its very embeddedness in a language, a history, and an economy seems irremediably particularized, however "expansively" one tries to speak its name, whether it is a matter of monotheistic revelation, democratic values, labor internationalism, or even demonstrative science *ordine geometrico*. For none of these things has ever been recognized everywhere or by everyone, and yet none of them is any longer restricted to a single region or a single "state." This also means that the discursive space of universalisms, of the historical enunciations of the universal, isn't rarefied; it has become *dense*. It isn't like Locke's "America," an ideal or fictional virgin space, but rather a Hobbesian "state of nature," where everyone faces off against everyone else and sees everyone else as rivals. Although obviously cultural and historical, the "natural" form of the relation of the universal to itself, at least as it pertains to discourse, is henceforth conflict and redundant multiplicity. *Not expressing the universal is impossible, but expressing it is untenable*; not doing so means being constantly bombarded by other enunciations. It is against this backdrop that I would now like to return to certain major philosophical debates connected to the eminently classical names of Hegel, Marx, and Freud.

The first debate, centered around several of Hegel's texts, concerns *the conflict of universalities*—or *conflicting universalities,* a term I borrow from Judith Butler.[4] The second, centered around the famous and enigmatic formula attributed to Marx—"the ruling ideology is the ideology of the ruling class"—concerns the relationship between the enunciation of the universal and the idea of domination or, more precisely, the relation between the dominant and the dominated. The third, which I will address much more rapidly but which is also the most difficult, focuses on Freud's theses on identification and ideality, which contemporary interpretations allow us to read in a new way. It concerns the relationship of the universal to the idea of community and the aporia of its deconstruction or critique.

I will begin with the conflict of universalities. In a sense, as I mentioned a moment ago, this situation of conflict is the most immediately obvious, the most easily perceived aspect of our relationship to discourses of the universal and what we are most accustomed to discussing. It offers a powerful argument in favor of relativism, which often appears, following a well-established skeptical tradition, in the form of a challenge to the *claims to universality* made by competing discourses, generally assumed to be underpinned by the interests of power or by the effects of custom and institutions. To quote Pascal: "Truth on this side of the Pyrenees, error on the other side."[5] Yet in quoting him, we mustn't forget the apologetic function of the aphorism, which is meant to disqualify the claim to universality of a properly human order of discourse in order to bring it back to the transcendental order of revelation and to the unique institutional tradition that reinforces it: "The history of the Church ought properly to be called the history of truth," writes Pascal in a fragment of the *Pensées*[6] that editors and critics have not been able to connect with any immediate context, perhaps because it governs the entire work.[7] For the Church, there are no Pyrenees, and more generally no frontiers, except those of the "provinces" of its orders. Now, this tradition has itself passed into the realm of finitude, of contingency, and thus of historical dispute. The "foundation" that it invokes now appears fragile.[8] The terminological nuance between *universal, universality,* and *universalism* is of some importance, and it may allow us to formulate more rigorously the solution that at first presents itself in order to situate the conflict between universalities within a teleology of the universal. The purpose, however, is not to refute that conflict but to find a way to define and affirm it. We must distinguish between the *universal* as such—by definition removed from the conflict, from the disputes and relativization that the latter entails—and the *universalisms* that constitute a claim to the universal, the universal's institutional effects, or its simulacrum in the field of opinion and belief. The Hegelian dialectic of the figures of spirit has sometimes been understood in this sense, as a means of transforming skepticism, the acknowledged relativity of enunciations of the universal, into a historical process, underpinned by the logic of universalization or, if one prefers, of real globalization, that gives it its meaning and finality.

Still, in this initial form, we are dealing more with a Platonic thesis than with a Hegelian one: *The universal* would here be the essence, or the absolute ("anhypothetical") event located beyond essence, which we may only ever be able to reach virtually. *Universalisms* would then be the "true opinions" that capture its reflection but at the same time dissolve its authenticity in the realm of appearances and individual interests that merely go unrecognized as such. We can apply a dialectic of this kind to the history of the conflict between the great religions or religious traditions that are specifically said to be "universal," all of which seem to associate, with or without proselytism, a principle of *uniqueness* with an opening to the *totality* of humanity. But at a second level we can also apply it to the eminently topical history of the conflict between *religious universalism* and *secular universalism*. The typically modern, Western form of secular universalism, constitutive of what we call *modernity* and that we readily take to be the heritage of the Enlightenment, combines the universality of the scientific method or "natural light," the universality of juridical rationality based on individual freedom and the equality of legal subjects before the law, and, finally, the cosmopolitical perspective of an extension of all these values to the whole of humanity. Lastly, we can apply the same dialectic of the retreat of the universal and the conflict of universalisms to the history of confrontations between the political ideologies of the modern era and in particular between liberalism and socialism, which are clearly two rival interpretations of classical cosmopolitism.

I am not by any means challenging a priori such a distinction between *the universal* and *universalisms*, at least as a working hypothesis. The distinction is perhaps as ineluctable as the opposition between truth and error or the real and the imaginary, and, in a way, it reproduces within historical universality (as its own specific "element") the logical opposition between the universal and the particular. However, it simultaneously perpetuates the same metaphysical presuppositions. This is why a more dialectical move would be to challenge the ontological difference between the *reality*— whether materialist or idealist—of the universal and the *appearance*, not to say imposture, of the universal inherent in universalisms, and thus to attempt to analyze *the differend of universalisms* as the very modality in which the historicity of the universal, or its constitutive *equivocity*, is given.

It is for this reason that several years ago I attempted to oppose an "extensive" universalism and an "intensive" universalism. On the one hand, I described an enunciation of the universal whose core idea is that a principle of right, salvation, justice, or culture must be *extended* to the whole of humanity, must reach its furthest *limits*, thus allowing humanity to unify and totalize itself (to "lose nothing" of itself, as it were) until it encompasses, as we know, an entire geography and cosmology of the human. On the other hand, I described an intensive enunciation, for which I gave the example (and it is perhaps much more than an example) of the proposition of equal liberty, or *equaliberty* in a single word, which corresponds to what Hannah Arendt calls the "right to rights"—in other words, a proposition that states that in a given political community, regardless of its size, the condition for the freedom of individuals and social groups, for *the absence of tyranny*, is their mutual equality, *the absence of privileges*, and vice versa, without it ever being possible to play these two principles off against each other or even rank them hierarchically.[9] I am not here to defend this idea for its own sake, an idea that I thought I could base on a certain *political* reading of the declarations of rights and revolutionary constitutions of the modern era. I offer it rather as an example of one way of dialecticizing the very concept of the universal, by moving beyond the simple opposition between true and false, between the truth of the universal and the appearances of competing universalisms. Some time afterward, I was very interested to discover a nearly homonymous opposition, albeit part of a completely different tradition, in the work of the American philosopher Michael Walzer. In a text from 1992 published in French under the title "Les Deux Universalismes," he draws on the example of the two currents of Judaism to oppose the messianism of the chosen people and the prophetism of justice, which he calls a "covering-law" universalism, virtually dominant and assimilatory, with a horizontal universalism, which would be immanent to every community but would also communicate with all the others, following the modality of the example or exemplarity rather than the vertical modality of assimilation.[10]

I don't really have the time to discuss this fascinating line of argument or to compare it with my own formulation or with others that are more or less equivalent, although I will perhaps do so one day. Instead, I would like now to take a further step, with the help of Hegel. Indeed, I believe that Hegel, especially in the *Phenomenology of Spirit*, which must be read as a veritable dialectic of enunciations of the universal and of their constitutive paradoxes, closely associated two theses whose conjunction is much stronger than these binary distinctions, whether Walzer's or my own. This is because he rigorously refused the possibility of metalanguage, the illusion of being able to position oneself beyond the discourses of the universal in order to evaluate and relativize them on the basis of an absolute criterion. He positioned himself, as a consequence, in the finitude of historical universality and the infinite succession of the figures of that finitude. Hegel's first thesis, as I recalled a moment ago, sets forth a devastating paradox: *By simply stating the universal*, or by speaking in the modality of the universal, one immediately, irremediably, finds oneself in extreme particularity. Indeed, the idea of an *absolute* enunciation, detached from its place, time, conditions, and thus from its determinations, is a contradiction in terms. But the universal does not exist *elsewhere*, prior to or beyond its enunciations (*epekeina tou logou*, if you will pardon the pastiche of Plato); it is nothing other than their effect or aim. To which we must immediately add Hegel's second idea: namely, that the typical form of particularization or determination of the universal is *conflict* and, ultimately, *the struggle to the death of competing enunciations of the universal*, of symmetrical and incompatible universalisms. Conflicting universalities in the strongest sense of the term.

This idea is developed throughout the *Phenomenology* in the analysis of consciousness and already, prior to that analysis, in the description of what we might call, following Benveniste, *the formal apparatus of the enunciation*. The latter refers to the double constraint that brings to bear on the subject the need to appropriate language and that brings to bear on language the need to pass through the enunciation of an individual or collective subject—which immediately entails that this same subject is at once, in a radical unity of opposites, absolutely particular and absolutely universal or universalizing.[11] Yet in a central section of his book, Hegel gives us the historically decisive version of the argument, where we see that the two theses are reflections of the same fate: the fate of the universal to be particularized whenever it is expressed and the necessary tendency of the universal to be realized in the conflict between systems of thought that are opposed in each of their terms. Each movement is the virtual destruction of the other; they are the two sides of the same phenomenon. This is in the section entitled "Spirit," which quickly becomes "Self-alienated Spirit," another name for what Hegel generally calls "culture" (*Bildung*).[12] We are already familiar with the two successive figures of the universal's antagonisms, the one ancient, the other modern, which are the extraordinary instruments of interpretation and critique with which we live intellectually and which I have always thought anticipate the situations, discursive constraints, and the political and theoretical stakes that define our own contemporary debates about universalism.

The first is the figure of conflict inherent in the relationship between Law and Power, or between Legitimacy and Effectivity, which Hegel, following the example of Sophocles' Antigone, locates in the context of the Greek city where the "birth of politics" occurred (Moses Finley). On the one hand, conflicting universalities here assume the form of the *laws of the city* or, to put it another way, the form of the city's "constitution of citizenship" (*politeia*), which politics has the role of enforcing, transcending particular interests in the name of the higher interests of the community of citizens (*polis*). On the other hand, they assume the form of what Antigone herself calls the "unwritten laws" (*agrapta nomima*), the ethical imperatives that are apparently founded in a particular feeling of brotherly love (*philein*) but that in reality aspire to the unconditional character of piety and humanity. In conflicting universalities, therefore, the very notion of *law* (*nomos, nomima*) is at stake, a notion split between the model of will and the model of fate. And as we already know, the conflict is irreconcilable, in which the universal is neither on one side nor on the other but on both sides at once, torn between the two as if between life and death.[13]

The second is the modern figure of the conflict between faith and reason, *Glauben* and *Vernunft*, the two antithetical figures through which the ideal of the education of humankind is realized and, by way of this *Bildung*, the ideal of the explanation and intelligibility of the social world. Hegel implicitly attaches faith to Christianity, and more specifically, as Jean Hyppolite, his first French interpreter and translator, judiciously shows, to its purified form during the Reformation, whereas he explicitly attaches reason—rationalist universality or universalism as rationalism—to the "Enlightenment."[14] These two figures, engaged in a life-and-death struggle throughout modernity, a modernity that we now know is anything but linear or irreversible, both aspire to *insight* into the world (the German term is *Einsicht*, which puts us in the visual realm, although we are obviously dealing with the *vision of spirit*). But they do so in radically opposite ways, such that each is the other's irreconcilable *other*, each the other's enemy: religious "superstition" on the one hand, bourgeois "materialism" or "utilitarianism" on the other. The first, the universality of faith, seems to possess the characteristics of what I earlier called an intensive universalism, rooted in self-referential subjectivity or even mysticism, while the second, *die Aufklärung*, aligns with extensive universality, encyclopedic knowledge, and cosmopolitical law. Both, however, work to disseminate a principle, whether of morality or civilization, and both aim to control the state and, more generally, the *institution* of society, the bonds of the spiritual "masses," of the generations, and of mutual recognition. They are the preeminent figures of institutional recognition through which consciousness becomes the immanence of society in the individual.[15]

I regret not being able to go into greater detail; the ideal would be to re-read Hegel's chapter and to unpack each of his allusions line by line. Instead, let us ask a simple question: What is *still missing* from this symmetrical presentation of the conflict of universals and of the conflictual essence of universalism in the version that the author of the *Phenomenology* proposes? Some would say: obviously, the overcoming, the "sublation" of the conflict (*die Aufhebung*), and here we would be back on familiar ground, at least if we indeed wanted to be good Hegelians, if we agreed to identify the very instance of truth with the teleology that leads to a certain conception of the State of Right and, thereby, to the ultimate realization of the universal in absolute spirit. To which others, reiterating their skepticism, would no doubt reply: Just look how these figures, or so-called figures, of the absolute are imbued with particularity, prejudices, Judeo-Christian, Eurocentric, or even colonial bias, etc. Hardly a day goes by that we don't see very good new work on just this topic.[16] But I will take a different path. Indeed, I would like to show, if only allusively, what deconstructs Hegel in Hegel, or what allows us to deconstruct him—which is not to invalidate him. I will focus on two elements in this regard. The first has to do with a philosophical affirmation that Hegel consistently makes: If there are figures of consciousness, which we recognize are nothing other than figures of the universal, this is not because everything takes place *within* consciousness nor, more precisely, *for* consciousness. On the contrary, it is because there is *a remainder of unconsciousness, Bewusstlosigkeit,* that remains inaccessible to it (Hegel says that the movement of sublation of the figures of consciousness, which is the result of their limitation itself, or of the gap that they are never able to fill between certainty and truth, occurs "behind their back").[17] And this remainder is ultimately essential: the very force and trace of the limitation constitutive of consciousness, the sign of its finitude, which results from its need to *represent* what it expresses in a determined way and thus to sacrifice the thing that moves it—namely, the infinite desire to know and appropriate the world. The other element, which may, at bottom, be the same as the first, has to do with the fact that the conflicts between ethical principles, civilizations, and political institutions to which Hegel refers are not and cannot be exhaustive. Above all, they cannot be wholly symmetrical. Here again we see the *remainder* emerge, albeit in a very strange, symptomatic way, at the limits of what Hegel says and does not say.[18]

Hegel thus presents the conflict inherent in the Greek city—between the law of the state, maintained by its magistrates, bearers of the *arche,* and the unwritten laws of *philein* or *piety*—as a conflict between two principles. He says a conflict between two "laws" or legitimacies; however, the conflict is borne by a woman, or more precisely a "sister," Antigone, such as the poet recreated her, and the commentary since Hegel has sufficiently demonstrated that the sex of this "virgin" woman can neither be neutralized nor ignored, neither abstracted nor essentialized.[19] It is this persistent *anthropological difference,* irreducible to the "complementarity" of genders, that bears the conflict within the universal, the universal thus constituting the *unconscious of consciousness* itself. But Hegel cannot put things in this way. And that explains why, at the end of his discussion of Antigone, in an *afterthought,* he makes a startling formulation, one destined to produce interminable effects beyond the confines of his text: The femininity of womankind (*die Weiblichkeit*—it isn't clear if he is still speaking of Antigone or if he has moved on from this specific, even monstrous, case to a kind of transhistorical genericity) is "the everlasting irony of the community" (*die ewige Ironie des Gemeinwesens*), which should be understood as both the *nuisance,* the killjoy, of the political community and, perhaps, its sole resource for effectively rising to the level of universality because of the challenge that it poses to the community's exclusions, social and political fetishes, and institutional violence, transforming it in the process into something akin to a "community without community."

But still more striking is the end point of Hegel's exposition of the conflict between Christian Faith and Enlightenment Reason.[20] Given the way in which he endeavors to stylize and order the series of principles upon which Western European societies were established, and given, a fortiori, the date that his work was written (1807), it is obviously impossible not to ask oneself what has happened to the most recent, the most remarkable, and the most topical of his enunciations of the universal, with which, as we know, he would always continue to grapple as he sought to dissociate its progressive, bourgeois aspect from its insurrectional, anarchistic, and disorganizing aspect—I am referring to the discourse of *human rights*. Without speculating pointlessly about Hegel's cautiousness or self-censorship, how are we to understand that this revolutionary discourse is literally excluded from the dialectic of the universal, whereas it is precisely this discourse that gives the universal its name, including for Hegel? We are confronted with a *Bewusstlosigkeit*, this time not of "consciousness" but rather of the author himself, the very same Hegel who, whenever he describes the movement of consciousness, never fails to observe a subtle balance between identification and distance.

And yet we need merely reread the text, in what you will, I hope, allow me to call a symptomatic way, to realize that this lacuna is a fiction: It isn't really a lacuna at all, or rather it is the product of a surprisingly radical decision (a gesture, truth be told, that Hegel would never repeat and that would remain, in his writing of the *Phenomenology*, absolutely unique). The universality of human rights and of their enunciation in the form of a declaration, which constitutes such a turning point in the history of the West (and perhaps beyond), is not described as a simple figure of historical consciousness: It is described as a figure of death or, if one prefers, it violently returns self-consciousness to its origin in a struggle to the death but in a way that is both nihilistic and *nonrepresentable*. This occurs in the section on the Terror, immediately following the *Aufklärung*, which completes the discussion of spirit, with respect to which it represents an absolute reversal—unless, that is, it is radically contesting the foregoing discussion's conclusions by exposing spirit to the abyss (*zugrunde gehen*).[21] The Terror is described as a rigorous fulfillment of Rousseau's ideas, a frenzy of equality, or, better, of equaliberty, in which the illusion of reconstructing society on the basis of a civic virtue that proceeds from reason but resembles faith leads to widespread suspicion, to the conversion of love and philanthropy into a desire to purify the community, a desire that continually creates an internal enemy in order to eliminate within that enemy all that hinders the fulfillment of the universal. The Terror, therefore, instead of leading to a "beautiful" death charged with collective symbolism—to a patriotism or messianism of freedom—results in a collapse of meaning. Hegel, we will recall, depicts the daily work of the guillotine, the ultimate egalitarian, humanist, and universalist instrument of execution, as the equivalent of a machete lopping off heads of cabbage in a field.[22]

But once again there are—at least "for us"—two ways to read this turn in Hegel's argument, one of the most provocative written with the ink of a philosopher's speculation. We can see it as the symptom of his prejudices, of his political positions, let us say, which were counterrevolutionary if not altogether reactionary, acquired in all probability at the cost of a harrowing disillusionment contemporaneous with events. Let us say, then, that because a struggle to the death underlies the conflict of universalities, a struggle that is of the order of life and not merely of representation, or that constitutes the remainder of a representation of the real, the recognition of the unconscious part of consciousness has as its corollary a resounding denegation of this unconsciousness, the political dimensions of which may here come fully into view: namely, the fact that conflictual universalities ultimately call into question the figures of domination and resistance themselves; they call into question the revolt of the masses against all forms of universality that coincide with their own exclusion, with their own invisibility to others and to themselves. And yet as soon as we present things in this way, we can see that there is still another reading of Hegel's argument, one that includes the recognition, albeit oblique, *by Hegel himself* of what I will venture to call a "denegatory" enunciation of the universal: The discourse of human rights, if sufficiently radical, *does not depend upon consciousness and its institutional "figures"* but always exceeds them. This is because of the risk the discourse presents, its potential for extreme violence, as well as its particular historical character, which transforms it into an act of insurrection and dissolution rather than of foundation and constitution. Such is obviously not the case with all varieties of statements having to do with human rights and the politics of human rights, which quite clearly belong entirely to the history of conflicts of the universal. However, such is the case with the "pure" statement of the proposition of equal liberty as a political principle: an enunciation approaching the inarticulable, because it must forgo invoking principles, generalities, revelations, and deductions, and because it is always reiterated, in very different epochs, in very different languages, and in words that are not strictly equivalent, not exclusively attached to any particular institution of universality, but that periodically come to mark the same point of heresy in which the limits of representation and the fault lines of domination intersect.

Now that, following Hegel, we have situated the ironic figure of Antigone on the margins of the laws of the ancient city and located the abyss of the Terror at the limits of the conflicts between modern faith and modern reason, it may be possible to describe somewhat better the dialectic of *conflicting universalities* in light of certain contemporary debates. Judith Butler herself seems to have espoused a pluralist perspective, which she reconceptualizes using the categories of "translation" and translatability.[23] To be sure, translation is not dialogue; it can be violent. Above all, it inevitably contains its share of the untranslatable. And this untranslatable bars us from formulating "positively" a common and consensual basis for emancipatory discourses that simultaneously involve heterogeneous, noncontemporaneous structures of oppression, structures whose negations accumulate on the same bodies and in the same souls but whose resistances and revolts, engendered by those structures, cannot purely and simply be *added up* in the name of the abstract universality of the defense of human rights. This is why Butler borrows Gayatri Spivak's description of the *double bind* that traps poor women of the Third World, the "subalterns" par excellence, who "cannot speak" ("the subaltern cannot speak," a remark whose irony mustn't be forgotten), for they are subjected both to colonial and postcolonial racism and to patriarchal sexism, and must therefore both make common cause with their men and radically dissociate themselves from them. This is also why Spivak, like Butler after her, turns to Lyotard's concept of the "differend," although she somewhat shifts its initial point of application: Expressions of the universal are not only in competition, in conflict, by the mere fact of their determination, of their inscription in history and institutions, they are, or ultimately become, heterogeneous as the repressed, the unconscious, of their own history returns within them. At the level of the institution, therefore, they reveal no preestablished synthesis but only usages, enunciations whose conservative or revolutionary, destructive or creative, effects depend upon the given moment.[24]

I have indulged in a long discussion of Hegel and, by way of Hegel, of this first aspect of the problem of enunciations in the modality of the universal. If we want to grasp the stakes of the problem, how could it be otherwise? Now, however, since this was only my first point, I obviously won't be able to "tackle" the other two in the same way; in fact, I am not going to tackle them at all. Instead, I will *say* what they are concerned with, from the perspective of ongoing work to which your invitation has returned my attention. And I will indicate why, *once again*, I have mentioned the names of Marx and Freud, and why, *once again*, I have done so in that order, with the example in mind of all those, including Althusser (but not only him), who have sought to link them together, or correct them using one against the other, while upholding, most often in the background or behind their backs, so to speak, a Hegelian position on the problem of universality in its relationship to domination and emancipation—or the class struggle in the general sense of the term—and to what Freud calls culture—that is, to the apparatus of repression of unruly drives that for him is necessary for the construction of a community. This will bring me back to the question of equal liberty and to the paradoxical modalities of its enunciation.

What Hegel calls consciousness, or, better, consciousness of the universal, Marx calls "ideology." *It is the same thing*, and yet this change in denomination, like the *Deus sive natura* of Spinoza (*conscientia sive ideologia*, I would suggest), opens the possibility of saying something new, or at least of putting at the forefront of the discussion that part of unconsciousness that Hegel constantly relegates to the margins of the phenomenological field. Obviously, we are talking about *domination* (*Herrschaft*, the word that Hegel associates with *servitude* or *Knechtschaft*) and the structural *violence* (*Gewalt*), whether visible or invisible, inseparable from domination. We know that Marx twice employs the term domination, or rather he reiterates it in a way that creates what appears to be a redundancy but is in fact a problem—perhaps the most difficult, the most nagging, the most insoluble, and also the most fertile of philosophical problems associated with Marxist thought and its critical legacy. Roland Barthes, as I was reminded by Tom

Conley, on whom I tested some of this evening's arguments, had the habit of saying in his lectures: "All ideology is dominant." Which means, tautologically, that it dominates, that it exists solely through its exercise and modes of domination, and that whatever does not dominate, whether discourse or consciousness, is not, strictly speaking, an ideology. Certainly, but what does ideology dominate? We often make do with the answer: individuals, groups, classes, but this clarifies nothing. Althusser attempted to improve upon this instrumental representation, arguing that what "dominant" ideology dominates is not people but always-already *subjected subjects*—in other words, another ideology, a "dominated" ideology, if you like, and, through this intermediary, the individuals that it constitutes as subjects. Except that the *dominated* ideology is invisible, nowhere to be found; it remains evanescent or virtual precisely because it is dominated.[25] As we know, Marx's expression is: "The dominant ideology is the ideology of the dominant class" (*The German Ideology*); for example, bourgeois ideology is the ideology of the bourgeoisie. We haven't found our way out of the tautology.

In reality, this tautology, or pseudo-tautology, conceals a profound dilemma, about which the descendants of Marx, and through him of Hegel, have remained divided. How should we speak of domination, how do we account for the violence of the universal, the violence that the universal allows one to exercise physically but also that it itself constitutes, and, ultimately, the counter-violence that it provokes, without describing the domination of the dominant ideology as an invasion or imposition from above, whether we are talking about class struggle, colonialization, and racism or sexism and homophobia, etc.? And how do we account for the fact that, when domination attains the universality without which it has no chance of fulfilling the function that Gramsci would later call "organic" or "hegemonic" in a given society, *the dominant ideology must speak the universal and not the particular, express the law in the modality of the universal or in the modality of the general interest and not that of privilege*? How do we account for this fact without also supposing that, historically and logically, the dominant ideology arises not from the ideas or values of *the dominant* but from *the dominated themselves*, the bearers of claims to justice, equality, freedom, emancipation, education, and so on? The question here has nothing to do with the sincerity or hypocrisy with which these values are asserted by those from above, but rather with the structural constraint that makes these values part of the inescapable language of domination—and we know, furthermore, that if the dominant didn't "believe" at all in that language, they wouldn't be able to put it to use. We must assume, therefore, that in addition to and beneath the economic mechanisms of exploitation there is something like an *expropriation of the ideology of the dominated by the dominant themselves*, of which multiple examples exist, from the great universalist religions of salvation to the revolutionary ideology of human rights. This may leave open the possibility of a performative reversal of the discourse of the universal, of turning it against its uses and functions of domination, but this also seems to bind it irreversibly to the limitations of a subaltern position, which eventual recourse to the "pure act," or to terror, does nothing to change—on the contrary.

At this point, we will have to make a detour to Freud. Not to his work in general but to the *late* Freud, who examined the individual's unconscious relation to what he calls the "masses" (*die Masse*) in *Group Psychology and the Analysis of the Ego* (1921) and in the texts on "culture" that run from *The Future of an Illusion* (1927) to *Civilization and Its Discontents* (1936) by way of "the invention of the *superego*," which he describes as the preeminent civilizing authority but also as the representative of the death drive in the psychic economy.[26] Shall we say that, under the name of culture, Freud presents the paradox (which here he calls the *discontent, das Unbehagen*) of universality for a third time, here locating its enunciation or injunction, instead of at the level of consciousness, at the level of the unconscious, in which the anthropological necessity of the institution is grounded? Since we have to proceed quickly, that is indeed what I will say. And I will draw your attention to two characteristics of his discourse. Freud is a political liberal, but his theses on groups and their relationship to culture and therefore to the universal are markedly conservative, haunted by the *fear* of the role the masses play in politics. This doesn't mean racist or nationalist. At the beginning of *The Future of an Illusion*, he explicitly distances himself from the Germanist ideology opposing *culture* and *civilization*, which someone like Thomas Mann still embraced at the time, albeit not for much longer.[27] Yet Freud holds that culture is necessary not only in order to compensate for the renunciation of infantile desires but also in order to inspire a love of work in people governed by the pleasure principle. He believes that these two necessities are at once more urgent and more difficult to fulfill in the case of the working classes, who don't enjoy the pleasures of "sublimation" (science and art) and are plagued by resentment toward the educated classes.

For them, culture is thus not a production in its own right but rather an external imposition, a double alienation. Hence the historical and political importance of religion, which represents precisely the form of sublimation of the instincts in which the fulfillment of infantile desire is the most completely preserved although at the same time transformed into collective messianic hope, to which Freud applies the specific term *illusion* (conscientiously avoiding the opposition between illusion and the real, the former opposed to the ascetism of knowledge and to the cult of doubt). Illusion is the Freudian *universal*, or rather illusion is one of its aspects.

Freud is thoroughly a man of the Enlightenment: He espouses the dialectic of faith and knowledge not only as two ethics but as two politics. Yet he is a radically pessimistic man of the Enlightenment. He sees contemporary humanity trapped between the decline of the universals of faith, which he thinks have been discredited or trivialized and thus have lost their cultural capacity among the masses, at least in the West, and the impotence of the universals of reason, in particular those of scientific reason, which he thinks, rightly or wrongly, and even if he mentions contemporary teaching experiments in passing (including those underway in the Soviet Union in the 1920s), lack the power to effectively destroy belief—in other words, they cannot substitute for the mechanisms of collective identification that develop and bind together *communities*.[28] These theses become clearer if we turn to his analyses from 1921 in *Massenpsychologie und Ich-Analyse*. I will limit myself to simply pointing out that in their description of the mechanisms of obedience to authority, his analyses very closely associate references to the charisma of leaders and references to the abstraction and universality of systems of ideas or, if you prefer, the universality of *ideologies*, whose fundamental characteristic in his eyes is that subjects relinquish their ability to make judgments about "reality," which then becomes entrusted to a personal or an impersonal Other. It is in this same context, explicitly discussing the Church and making a transparent allusion to contemporary revolutionary parties, that Freud emphasizes the presence of a constitutive tension within the mechanism of collective identification between its *authoritarian* dimension and *egalitarian* dimension. Admittedly, though, the latter seems to be radically divorced from the idea of emancipation and set more squarely on the side of voluntary servitude.

This means that Freud conceived of *a third characteristic of enunciations of the universal*, which not only includes *conflict*, as in Hegel, and *domination*, as in Marx, but the formation of an *ideal of the community* (one is tempted to say, a "we ideal," just as he conceived of an "ego ideal") that involves all the mechanisms of repression and sublimation of love and death drives that traverse the community. Rousseau already recognized as much: The universal is not the mere *representation* of a unified community but rather its *idealization*, through which the community is realized and institutionalized as an "indivisible" bond between those who gather together, obey the same leaders, and believe in the same dogmas, as well as between those who revolt against the same authority or fight for the same justice. These are obviously not the same discourses, the same emblems, the same names of the universal (although most of the truly effective, meaningful names are in fact equivocal, constantly appropriated and expropriated by antagonistic forces). For the third time, and not by chance, we encounter the idea of the *differend*. We know all too well that there is no unequivocal, definitive way of creating the *differend* or of deconstructing the being of the community in the element or modality of the universal. Term-by-term reversals are not enough, nor are transgressions, but neither are pure and simple substitutions of one universal for another—for example, that of the market, exchange, equivalence, or mutual obligations for that of the cultural community; or that of the dominant universality of the market for that of communism or fraternity. The "community without community" to which the philosophers of deconstruction refer (Blanchot, Derrida, Nancy), which may be nothing other than the "community without the ideal of community" or the being in common without the "we," nonetheless also partakes of an ideal or perhaps a *gamble*: that of a *suspension of* domination or of a liberation from illusion in the Freudian sense. It thus remains a problem, not a solution, and still less a prescription. And it is more interesting that way, because much more difficult.

3

SUB SPECIE UNIVERSITATIS

Speaking the Universal in Philosophy

The French-Latin wordplay that makes the term *universitas* into the origin of both *university* and *universality* is obviously anything but accidental.[1] Philosophers, or certain of them, have been eager to use it whether in a spirit of critique or self-promotion to think about the status of their discipline. Since philosophy became an essentially academic specialization, not only has it never stopped thinking of itself as the field in which one seeks to elucidate the conditions and effects of a discourse of the universal, but universality has become the *objective value* from which it derives its legitimacy. Skeptical or deconstructionist discourses don't contradict this characterization, although they might impose limitations on the possibility of knowing, stating, fulfilling, and transmitting the universal or adopt a *negative* point of view with regard to these objectives. In philosophy, to take an anti-universalist position and to consider philosophy as the overcoming, critique, or deconstruction of universalism is *still* "to state" the universal in a certain *modality*, which can be a way of preserving it. To take such a position is as a result to put oneself in a cyclical rather than dialectical movement that perpetually revives the universal as positivity.

To this preliminary remark, I will add a second: Understood as "university" and as "universality," the category of *universitas* always contains the idea of a *totality*. Think of the familiar expressions from classical and scholastic Latin: *universitas rerum, universitas generis humani, universitas studiorum*. Indeed, "universities" were created in parts of the West with the ambition of leaving no domain of knowledge beyond the scope of their program of study (although this immediately poses the question of what "knowledge" is, knowledge in the fullest sense of the term—an object of *theoria* and *mathesis*), and thereby of including everything that speculatively concerns humanity. In the modern era, philosophy has not only been intimately linked with this project, it has undertaken to define the guiding idea and the conditions of the project's institutional realization.[2]

Still, this reciprocity of determinations has always had its problems, today more than ever. No doubt one of the objectives that philosophers should collectively set themselves is to problematize the state of their discipline anew, at the point where *universitas* as institution and *universitas* as logical and ontological category intersect. We have good reason to believe—and even more so than at the time of Husserl's famous 1935 lecture on "Philosophy and the Crisis of European Man"—that this intersection is neither natural, inevitable, or irreversible. It may well be that in the future (if such is not already the case) "universities" or "grandes écoles" will have no need of a discipline "specialized in generalities," as Auguste Comte put it, to reflect on the classification of sciences and techniques (among which the techniques of communication, education, and the control of opinion). This isn't enough to make the crisis of the university a *philosophical* problem, but it may be a sufficient reason for professional philosophers to discuss the origins and symptoms of the crisis.

We should recall here once again that philosophy has not always been a university discipline, that it has perhaps never been one completely, and that given these circumstances it is by no means certain that it will remain one. What would then become of its "orientation toward the universal" or toward "the idea of the universal"? Before the nineteenth century, few philosophers were academics, whether or not they were ever offered university positions in the field. The glaring exceptions were in medieval universities, which, even so, continued the heritage of schools and intellectual communities where philosophy was studied at the same time as mathematics, music, medicine, or law. It is important to keep in mind that certain definitions or models of *universality* from which we still draw inspiration were not only not forged at the university but were forged *against it*. This was the case with the rationalist idea of *mathesis universalis* envisaged and given impetus by Descartes in the seventeenth century, and it was also the case with its empiricist antithesis, "natural history," in the broad sense the category acquired in the writings of Locke, Diderot, and Kant. Closer to our own day, discourses profoundly revitalizing the meaning and value of universalism have been formulated outside or on the margins of the university thanks to the intellectual activity of its outcasts or child prodigies—think of Kierkegaard, Emerson, Marx, Nietzsche, Tolstoy, Benjamin, Sartre, or even Wittgenstein.

It goes without saying that too many examples go in the diametrically opposite direction to allow us to conclude that, as a general rule, philosophy is invented *outside*, then developed, interpreted, historicized, systematized, and transmitted *inside* the university, as we are generally ready to admit for art and literature but also in large part for law and technology. Over the long term, however, the tensions appear sufficiently strong between these two poles to caution us against the illusion that the "place of the universal" or of reflection on the universal is quite so naturally *the institution that bears its name*. Now, this problem has more than administrative or sociological repercussions. First of all, it concerns the *styles*, or, if you prefer, the "language games," associated with certain institutional spaces and therefore with specific *practices* of reflection, writing, argumentation, and communication within institutions. I am not implying that universities impose on philosophical discourse a *single* mode of exposition, if only because of the very deep cleavages between national traditions within formally similar university institutions from one country to another, even though there is in fact a close relationship between the university framework, claims about "foundation" or "reflectivity," and the project of *universalizing* certain styles and according them a normative value. Nor am I simply predicting that the discursive styles or forms that in philosophy have been progressively excluded or marginalized by the institution, such as the poem, novel, dialogue, meditation, demonstration *ordine geometrico*, pamphlet, or manifesto, are now going to *make a comeback* in a "postuniversity" age of philosophy, the existence of which we have no way of guaranteeing, anyway. And yet this is certainly a sufficient reason to include in any discussion of the present and future of philosophy a reflection on the discursive norms and forms that philosophy has appropriated in virtue of its place within the university, with the aim in doing so of saying precisely what the universal is within the field of universality.

What makes such a reflection so overdetermined today is that its urgency and import come to us refracted through the prism of "geophilosophical" considerations (to repeat the expression employed, in contexts independent of one another, by Deleuze and Guattari and by Derrida and Nancy) whose frame of reference is at once geopolitical and geocultural.³ This is the consequence of a phenomenon of gradual relativization affecting a "culture," or "civilization," that, although it did not strictly speaking *invent* the university-form of knowledge, refined and imposed it on the entire world in the name of its values and with the help of its "universally valid" technologies (I am obviously speaking of the Western world, even if we would be hard pressed to fix its boundaries in any definitive way). We are henceforth asked to think of philosophy as a typically *Western* project, in other words, to recognize that there is a contradiction between what is essentially *local*, and thus "particular," about its methods and styles of thought, or more profoundly its *categories*, and what is *global* about its ambitions, especially with regard to the possibility of defining the general framework of a comparison between cultures. While it may be overly simple to present the contradiction in this way, the severity of the conflict it expresses can no longer be ignored, as François Jullien's work in particular has shown.⁴ The difficulty stems from the fact that we cannot avoid circularity when asking, as we often do, whether or not there is "philosophy," or "philosophies," outside Western culture (which happens to be—not coincidently, perhaps—the same culture devoted to the propagation of Hellenic influences and monotheistic religions).⁵ But it seems to me that the conflict cannot be overcome by following either of the two most common strategies: neither the first, which, however subtly, espouses the Eurocentric tradition of philosophies of history, continuing the secularization of the theological principle of election—that is, the idea that history is supposed to have produced, through miracles or necessity, *the local conditions for the emergence of the universal as such*, its *situs* or *topos* proper; nor the second, which, inversely, asks us to acknowledge that the very category of the universal is underpinned by a *universalist illusion*, that it is inseparable from the functions of domination or power that it fulfills, and thus from the *exclusions* or *repressions* that it justifies through arbitrary choices or violent degradations.

Rather than choose between these two symmetrical attitudes, I believe that we must get to the heart of the paradox enveloped in the hypothesis of a conjuncture or process of "real universalization"—in other words, of globalization, whose main unsettling effect has been to undermine the *representation of the universal* dominant in Western history and internalized by philosophers regardless of the tradition or school to which they belong—whether transcendental or dialectical philosophy, positivism, or analytic philosophy, etc. In other words, we will have to reflect on the fact that certain typically "Western" institutions, among which the university but also the market, technology, and administration, have become more and more widespread just as the "grand narratives" that legitimate them have become less and less influential. To succeed in this, we will naturally have to take a decentered approach that confronts several heterogeneous points of view; our reflection will thus have to include a moment of *conflict*, without which it will do nothing to alter our notion of *universitas* or to change the mirror that *universitas* holds before us. The "language" in which our reflection will appear remains unknown, or rather it will only emerge within the confrontation itself.

Finally, what seems to complicate any reflection on the *topos* or "site" of philosophy is that the project of developing a universal discourse on the universal—what I will take the liberty of calling *speaking the universal*—from within the "universalist" institution par excellence (the University or Academy) has always been contested. Not only has philosophy had "rivals," but through its confrontation with them it has acquired the certainty of speaking the universal in its own specifically "philosophical" way. Here we recognize the problem that Kant describes in *The Conflict of the Faculties*, written at a time when our current disciplines were in the process of acquiring their modern status (1798). Kant presents philosophy as a "lower" discipline, which was then competing with theology, law, and medicine to define the "ends" or ultimate questions of humankind (enumerated in the first *Critique*: What can I know? What ought I to do? What may I hope?). But since philosophy is in his eyes the sole discipline that addresses these ends according to purely rational principles (and not on the basis of revelation, authority, or empirical practice), it is philosophy's task to set the limits of validity to the ends determined by the "higher" faculties (the salvation of the soul, the rights and duties of the citizen, the healthy life, etc.) by opening within itself a region where they would become the object of a universally acceptable critical examination. In this way, philosophy wouldn't rule over the other disciplines as theology once "reigned" in medieval universities,[6] it would indirectly determine their theoretical and practical limits (which is also crucial for their *public* recognition). Today, we are forced to acknowledge that this conflict of the faculties has never disappeared but has instead assumed different forms, wherein the position "antagonistic" to philosophy has been held by numerous disciplines, from mathematics and logic to linguistics, from history to economics, from physics to biology and psychology. It sometimes seems as if philosophy has only kept its unique place because other paradigms of knowledge have had to fight among themselves to define the criteria of the "essential science."

What makes these conflicts so difficult to resolve and yet so essential to the renewed interest in the problem of universality (and in the *redefinition* of its content) is that the *boundaries* are never obvious (nor were they any more obvious for theology, law, or medicine at the beginning of the modern era). It is never possible to decide in any definitive way whether philosophy is the discipline that reflects (in a transcendental manner) on the principles, semantics, foundational problems, and practical aims of certain other disciplines, or if it is instead one of these universal forms of knowledge that provides philosophy with its questions and models of reasoning, or that *makes use of philosophy as an instrument* for its own conceptual clarification. In other words, from the point of view of philosophy, it is impossible to decide whether its essence is *in se* or *in alio*. Both enable us to grasp its specific (and privileged) relationship to the enunciation of universality, but in completely different styles and with completely different contents depending on the option we choose. If we turn to the recent past, we can surely agree that Heidegger, Sartre, and Bertrand Russell, or Freud, Max Weber, and Quine were all philosophers, albeit manifestly not in the same immediate sense (or only in an extremely trivial sense: All of them sought and used "abstractions"). I don't see any reason to believe that such conflicts and confrontations between different discourses *sub specie universitatis*, or between different enunciations of the universal represented by different disciplinary models, will stop influencing the conception that philosophy—playing both judge and judged—has of itself. Nothing, however, guarantees that these conflicts will take place within the framework of the University or that these enunciations will be resolved within the form of a concerted (and, in practice, hierarchical) system of academic disciplines.

To provide the discussion with a more specific framework, I would now like to compare *different philosophical strategies* that have been imagined within the Western tradition (if not in the Western university tradition) in order to resolve the paradoxes involved in the enunciation of the universal. Although their roots lie in the history of philosophy itself, these strategies also represent "critical" attitudes within philosophy. I will give a brief overview of three of them that to my mind continue to be essential. They are no doubt not the only strategies, but I have chosen them because they offer clear-cut orientations. My approach follows from the fact that, in a quite fundamental way, I don't believe that it is sufficient for philosophy simply to examine how it came to claim the role of speaking the universal, and to be institutionally legitimized in that role, nor for it simply to speculate about the contingent factors informing such a situation, or about the eventual reversal or disappearance of those factors. The greatest challenge for philosophy lies in the trope of *self-legitimation.* The conceptual *difficulties* raised by this trope—but at the same time its productivity, its capacity to cause unforeseen developments—call for a reexamination that will prepare philosophy for new intellectual adventures.

STRATEGIES OF DISJUNCTION

The first is the Spinozist-Wittgensteinian strategy. It goes without saying that Spinoza and Wittgenstein are very different thinkers (although some have tried to "read them together," not only on technical points such as the identification of truth with unique propositional contents that are by themselves their own "norm" or "criterion," but also from a more general perspective, particularly on the basis of their rejection of methodological and metalinguistic considerations in philosophy as well as their shared belief that no "super-concepts" exist).[7] But on the question of the universal they seem to me to share a typically *dualistic,* or better *disjunctive,* approach, in the sense that they distinguish between a "theoretical universalism" and a "practical universalism" whose languages are to a certain extent radically incompatible. One of these universalisms speaks a language of explanation and representation (or description), the other speaks a language of norms, effects, and uses. It is assuredly the task of philosophy to make these two languages communicate. But since there is nothing in this approach resembling an *external* (ideal or transcendental) *point of view* from which the difference could be reduced (or from which, and this amounts to the same thing, it could be viewed as a distribution of complementary "domains," like "nature" and "freedom" in Kant), philosophy becomes the art of describing or inventing paths from one "place" (*topos*) to the other, neither *really* being separate from the other (that is, they don't belong to different "worlds") yet remaining *qualitatively* (one is tempted to say *modally*) distinct. In other words, philosophy becomes the art of understanding why we still inhabit the same ("immanent") world in two contradictory ways that are nonetheless *both universalist*.

What gives additional relevance to the analogy (and makes it intellectually exciting) is that Spinoza and Wittgenstein were both led by the vicissitudes of their philosophical lives to write two different books, each of which, in its specific style and with its specific objectives, expounds from its own point of view (or language) one of these two forms of universality and reveals, for precisely this reason, its inability to address its antithesis except in the aporetic form of an *internal limit* or vanishing point whose significance can only be described *negatively*. This is clearly an uncomfortable situation, particularly so for philosophers who claim to be systematic, and we shouldn't be surprised when we discover them trying to resolve or dissolve the problem by introducing various mediations (by "translating" one problem into the language of the other: In Spinoza, it is apparently the problem of practice that is ideally translated into the language of theory; in Wittgenstein, it is instead the problem of theory that is translated into the language of practice—although in both authors, this is only a first step). Rather than discussing these mediations (these "systems"), I would like to focus on the aporia itself, which to my mind constitutes the most crucial aspect.

Spinoza wrote the *Ethics* in secret, a work that is essentially the construction of a form of intellectual life based on an understanding of the causal relations that exist among all natural individuals (including humans). Yet he published (albeit anonymously) the *Tractatus Theologico-Politicus*, which is a historical and philological discussion of the possibility of liberating the political community from a specific form of religious faith in order to reestablish it based on the free contributions of different faiths to the recognition of the common good or utility. Wittgenstein, on the other hand, published the *Tractatus Logico-Philosophicus*, which is an attempt to define the "logic" or "language" (*die Sprache*) common to all descriptions of the world (the most precise of which are scientific descriptions) as a totality of observable "material facts" (*Tatsachen*) or of actually existing relations between things (*Sachverhalte*). Yet he wrote (or drafted) the *Philosophical Investigations* in private, a text in which the object of his reflections is no longer the logical form identically present in the relation between empirical states of affairs and in their linguistic image or description (an idea that offers striking analogies with what has been called the parallelism of things and ideas in Spinoza), but rather the infinite variety of language games (*Sprachspiele*) through which "public groups" (that is, communities in a very broad sense, whether durable or ephemeral, built on the possibility of sharing certain meanings or interpretations), by following tradition as well as inventing new rules derived from practice (*Praxis*), learn to give expression to life or to transform experiences into words.[8]

In Spinoza, the theoretical universal is called *Deus sive Natura*, and it is explained by *the infinite chain of causal* (or *"productive"*) *relations between things* (including ideas) and by the impossibility of contingency (see *Ethics* I, Prop. 28–29). In Wittgenstein, it is called "the general form of the truth-function" (*Tractatus*, Prop. 6), and it is presented ("shown") as the complete system of operations that make the truth of a proposition, or its correspondence with reality, depend to a greater or lesser degree of probability (in the limit case, of certainty) on the truth of other subordinate propositions. The practical (or better, pragmatic) universal in Spinoza is called the "free state" or "free republic" and is defined as the possibility that heterogeneous (or even incompatible) doctrines or beliefs, rooted in different ways of *imagining* the situation of human beings in the world and of assigning them *ends*, contribute subjectively to the realization of a common objective or provide subjects with individual *motives* for making themselves useful to one another. In Wittgenstein, the practical universal figures in a more virtual fashion, in the way in which "everyday language" (which is nothing other than the sum total of all its uses) functions in practice as the condition of possibility for the establishment of "conventions" and aims, in particular, to regulate heterogeneous or conflictual forms of life.

At the conceptual level, we can see that these two universalities follow different schemas: One is constructed on the ideal unification of the multiplicity of experiences (even if in the form of an open, infinite or expanding unity, such as the one designated by the concept *nature* in Spinoza), whereas the other is built on the practical equivalence established by convention between a multiplicity of convictions or beliefs, thereby attesting to their irreducibility to any simple or unequivocal *representation*. This equivalence can itself be conceived only as a practical datum (that is, as a *contingent*, fragile, or reversible result of the common actions that it makes possible, a retroactive effect that does nothing to strip it of its reality but transforms it into a self-sustained dynamic process).

Finally, we can see that the movement in both Spinoza and Wittgenstein from one type of universality to the other remains paradoxical and can only really be described as a negative presentation of one type in the language of the other. This points to a deeply *skeptical* element in their work—skeptical but no less real, although probably less frequently identified in Spinoza than in Wittgenstein (because Wittgenstein would explicitly exchange his initial "dogmatism" for an apparent "relativism," whereas Spinoza, in the view of those initiated into his "esoteric" doctrine, employed more approximate language in the *Tractatus Theologico-Politicus* to make himself intelligible to the greatest number of readers). Not surprisingly, it is also at this point that the most considerable difficulties arise concerning the representation of the subject or agent. Some have said (perhaps ironically) that the subject constitutes a mystical element in Wittgenstein's *Tractatus* because, in terms of giving an adequate image of the material world, it can only feature as the ineffable correlate of the totality of logical language. But this *mystical* element is also *practical*; it coincides with the "gesture" of showing (*zeigen*) logical form, and it therefore possesses, in the analysis of "rules" and "games" in the *Philosophical Investigations*, an equivalent that has nothing mystical about it whatsoever: On the contrary, it belongs to the everyday experience of learning (since the operations of logic themselves comprise a language game, they *must be learned*, they belong to the realm of custom and tradition, which does not mean that their content is itself conventional or malleable).[9] In Spinoza, I would say that the problem becomes inevitable at the end of the *Ethics*, when the figure of the "wise man" (*sapiens*) emerges as a thinking subject who, having progressed through the three kinds of knowledge, is now liberated from the illusion of free will and capable of linking each singularity (including himself, as body and mind) to a causal necessity. But in *what world* does such a wise man live or exist? Since Spinoza does not believe in "other worlds," it cannot be outside the current world, but nor can it be in our "common" social world, where transindividual relationships are based on language and imagination. Unless we assume (an oblique solution suggested in the *Tractatus Theologico-Politicus*) that the wise man is capable of representing his science or wisdom, along with its anthropological implications, in the form of a *vera religio*, a "true religion" or "universal faith" in which *natura* is "retranslated" as *Deus* (an operation that, for Spinoza, as for many of his contemporaries, amounted to extracting the social and moral principles common to all historical monotheisms).

Now, this is more of a working hypothesis than a demonstration, and it should in my opinion lead us to stress the insurmountable *equivocity* of the concept of the universal in both authors—and more generally in all those authors to whose work we might apply, despite its uncertain history, the theory of "double truth."[10]

But isn't it precisely in this equivocity that the great interest and power of such constructions lie? Even their skeptical side is important here. Rather than pushing us to abandon the idea (or ideal) of universality, they show us that the idea can be defended in theory *and* in practice. On the other hand, they rid us of the illusion that we might derive "universal forms of life" from scientific knowledge of the world, and that, whatever the theory or doctrine may be, the rules of equivalence between "subjectivities" (and thus coexistence, common action, the production of a "common good," the practical resolution of conflicts) could be anything other than conventions and institutions. This also means that *universal institutions*, or at least the will to work toward universal institutions, indeed constitute a relevant political project—which may prove useful therapy against apocalyptic thinking. "Universal" here means, in an equivocal way, *convention* as well as *nature*, *contingency* as well as *necessity*, but each according to an entirely distinct modality.

STRATEGIES OF SUBSUMPTION

I would now like to describe a completely different strategy, one that also aims at demonstrating that the paradoxes of universality have an intrinsic character, but that situates them on a different level and steers us toward very different conclusions. I will call it the *Hegelian-Marxist* strategy because it was developed by Hegel (especially, if not exclusively, in the *Phenomenology of Spirit*, whereas his later works speak a profoundly different language in addressing the question) in terms of "consciousness" (and figures of consciousness) and "antagonism" (or conflictual recognition) before being reformulated by Marx in terms of "ideology" and "ideological domination." Each of these terminologies allows us to highlight certain implications of the problematic (which originally belongs to the realm of "German Idealism," with its dramatic theoretical and political reversals, but which has much broader significance and sheds light on some of the deepest problems of the dialectical tradition in general). To put things much more simply, it

seems to me that the underlying idea is the following: There can be no universality in the realm of ideas or representations (which in this case includes
actions and practices, since there can be no human or historical practice
without a representation, not only "for others" but also "for itself," *für sich*)
except *as a form of domination over other ideas and representations* (which
are then suppressed or relegated to minority status, pushed to a subaltern
position or the excluded status of the particular, if not the "tribal"). *Universality and hegemony* here become equivalent. Inversely, no ideology (no system of representations, no figure of consciousness) can attain universality
if it fails to function as a process of domination, if it fails to become a "dominant ideology" (*herrschende Ideologie*). We are dealing with an extremely
critical theory at which many have taken umbrage (and which has thus been
aggressively contested, particularly by "dogmatic" philosophers and thinkers, partisans of *absolute universalist discourses*, be they religious or secular, moral or scientific). The theory proved unwieldy even for its inventors
(especially for Marx and his disciples, who struggled desperately against the
idea, or perhaps the obvious fact, that their own discourse could only become universal, as a language of social emancipation, by establishing a form
of "domination" in its turn). However, it is less the ironic effect that interests me here than the conceptual structure of the argument itself.

I will begin with what we might call the Hegelian paradox of the universal: that is, the idea, present throughout the *Phenomenology*, that due to an
intrinsic limitation, or rather to an internal contradiction, *it is impossible
to speak the universal without immediately transforming it into a particular
discourse (or a particular representation)*—in other words, into its opposite.
The universal must indeed be spoken (or stated), even if only in an internal
or self-referential dialogue: It is by nature a discourse, or a moment in the
development of discourse, and it must be expressed by a subject of some
kind. As we know, Hegel vigorously challenged the notion that there might
be "ineffable" or "inexpressible" ideas or experiences (which the first chapter of the *Phenomenology* ridicules as the myth or mysticism of the *Un-
aussprechliche*), although that doesn't mean that everything can be said
immediately or in the *same* discourse by *a single* subject. On the contrary,
there exists a formal constraint inherent in language that prohibits expressing universality without making it the expression of the limits of *this* particular place and *this* particular time, and above all without restricting it to
the confines of a certain *point of view* intrinsic to the given situation. A his-

toricist reading of the thesis would point to Hegel's own later formulation (in the preface to the *Philosophy of Right*), "no one can overleap his own time" (or, no doubt, his own environment, although for Hegel environments are meaningful only insofar as they represent successive "sites" for the development of the *Weltgeist*), as a "factual" proposition that conveys the finitude of historical individuality. But Hegel's originality is to place universality at a deeper ontological level by describing it as a consequence of the structure of consciousness—in other words, by thinking universality as a category of conscious representation as such (the exact opposite, it so happens, of Wittgenstein or Spinoza). "Consciousness," as Hegel describes it phenomenologically—moving from *perception* (which can be attributed to an individual or an isolated consciousness) to the collective historical figures of *spirit* (today we would instead speak of *culture*, with all its institutional and political dimensions, as the structuring principle of communities)—is the faculty of thought (which Hegel immediately links with the faculty of speech[11]) that constructs *totalities of meaning* and endows them with certainty (*Gewissheit*) and truth (*Wahrheit*)—in short, with universality (*Allgemeinheit*). But consciousness can do so only from a specific point of view, precisely because it allows a plurality of individuals to share the same subjectivity (or allows individual or collective subjects, "I" and "we," to trade places: "'I' that is 'We' and 'We' that is 'I'"[12]). Consequently, what consciousness is directed at in each of its figures is not "the world" as such, but, each time, "its world," or a shared vision of the world, whose consistency comes from the intention of consciousness to project onto the totality of experience a principle of certainty or determinate truth (which can be epistemological, aesthetic, religious, juridical, etc.) and is, strictly speaking, only valid "for itself." The general idea that we cannot speak *sub specie universitatis* without immediately particularizing the universal that we are expressing (that is, without transforming it into its logical opposite) stems from the fact that every discourse or enunciation of the universal is subject to the law of conscious representation—in other words, there is universality only *for a consciousness* in this broad sense. And there is no consciousness without its intrinsic limits—that is, without its *conditions of possibility*.

It isn't difficult to see here a generalization of the Kantian idea of transcendental consciousness as the a priori form of organization of experience, on the one hand, and an unyielding critique of its claim to stand above experience itself, on the other. Even still, the argument is by no means relativist.

Consciousness and the language it speaks (for example, the moral language of responsibility and duty, the scientific language of causality, or the juridical language of freedom and equality) organize experience from within (from within in its own "history"); they must therefore dissolve (or combine) the opposites, the particular and the universal. The only way to avoid this constraint is by understanding the necessary transition from one figure of consciousness to another—that is, by understanding the principle of *historicity* immanent to their limitation (which is not a new figure of consciousness or another representation of the universal but the self-reflection or *naming* of this transition).

Nor is it difficult to understand how this description of consciousness and its paradoxical relationship to language—which at once particularizes and universalizes representations—could engender the Marxist notion of ideology. To be sure, the Hegelian figures of consciousness cover a wider range of experiences and meanings (encompassing not only social discourses—that is, those tied to certain dominant forms of society and politics—but also other types of worldviews: the mechanistic "laws" of nature, "religious revelations," etc.). Yet the Marxian interpretation of the communitarian dimension of representations (that is, their function of mediating between "I" and "We," between individual subjectivities and collective subjectivities) as the expression of historical class struggles draws our attention to the essentially *conflictual* nature that already constitutes a *general characteristic* of universality in its Hegelian determination. In fact, what Hegel wants to show is not simply that stating the universal forces a speaker or speakers to give the universal a particular form, but that doing so asserts one universality *against another*—and thus deprives the latter of its own universality, denies that it can be universalized. Not only does the universal represent a paradoxical unity of logical opposites, but it exists exclusively in the form of *universalities in conflict* (which can also be understood as the expression of competing interests, which Hegel relates to a general conception of life and spirit and Marx to a more specific concept of social production) struggling to establish their domination.

But what does "establish their domination" mean? It means that one discourse relativizes another, that it sets the criteria and defines the norms according to which the latter receives a limited value and function, is validated or invalidated—a hierarchical relation that in certain cases appears reversible, as in the famous Master-Slave dialectic, where the Slave's worldview, based on the universal value of Labor, ends up overturning the domination of the Master's worldview, which is based on the universal value of Sacrifice, thus transforming negativity into positivity and enabling the development of culture. But above all it means that a dominant discourse is a discourse that *reflects in itself the contradiction with its "other"* and makes this reflection the intrinsic impetus of its own development (still another idea that is not only a key to history but also reflects an ontological structure of consciousness). Certain famous passages of Hegel's *Phenomenology* provide a striking illustration of this principle. The most well-known is perhaps (and not by accident) the dialectic of "culture" itself (*Bildung*), in which Hegel describes the conflict between two great "universalities," the universality of Faith (in the theological sense) and the universality of secular Reason (in the form given to it by the *Aufklärung*), and which he presents as a scission of pure intellection (*Einsicht*): Reason, in order to appear universal to itself, presents Faith as "superstition," simultaneously appropriating the notion of certainty or belief produced by its other (by opposing the universality of rational beliefs to the particularity of superstitious beliefs, which also means by opposing the self-critical character of Reason to the noncritical character of Faith). But there are other no less striking examples, such as the dialectic of the Two Laws (that is, the conflict between the two absolutes of human morality and civic legality) in the history of the Greek city as it plays out in the tragedy *Antigone*; or the dialectic of Christianity as the religion of the Death of God, in which the principle of "picture-thinking" (*Vorstellung*), a principle originating in "natural religions" (polytheism, in which the divine is represented by individual figures), is realized only to be denied or sublimated spiritually in the idea of the Incarnation. We could find similar examples in *The Communist Manifesto*, which describes "social and communist doctrines" as the imaginary reversal of private property within the very heart of the dominant (liberal) ideology, an idea that would return in *Capital* in the form of the "abolition of capital within the confines of the capitalist mode of production itself"—a kind of *socialism within capitalism*.[13]

Once again, there is a strongly critical emphasis in these philosophical constructions. I don't view them as purely negative, however (such an interpretation, pushed to the extreme, would lead to the idea of a "negative dialectics," in which the universal represents the fetish, the abstraction, or the negation of the contradiction, which prevents us from thinking in terms of concrete singularities), but rather as *conceptual constructions of the universal*, which reveal its constitutive tensions or conflicts. And this brings me to a final consideration. In Hegelian-Marxian terms (or in the terms of the Marx who extends and displaces the phenomenological moment in Hegel), the *conflictual character* of universality does not represent a defect, a failure of universal discourses, but rather a *criterion* that allows us to identify those that truly deserve the name by exposing their ability to represent within themselves their other (or their adversary, their "enemy"—"superstition," in Hegel's description, being the Enlightenment's *Feind*) as the negative element that they require for their own development or to attain self-consciousness. In this sense, not only does conflict always exist wherever there is self-affirmation of the universal (all self-affirmation is in fact a hetero-affirmation), but the conflict is always *asymmetrical*, unequal, with a dominant, repressive side and a dominated, repressed side.

At this point, divergent interpretations are possible that obviously don't lead to the same practical conclusions. For the sake of simplicity, I will formulate these interpretations in quasi-strategic terms (which also seems justified by the fact that most of the examples in Hegel as well as in Marx have to do with historical or transhistorical conflicts between antagonistic worldviews). If one discourse of the universal dominates another (whether one calls it "consciousness," to indicate its ability to fashion subjectivities, or "ideology," to underscore its social function), this may mean that the dominated discourse has no choice, in order to express its difference or resistance, but to fall back on the logic, categories, and rhetoric of the dominant discourse—that is, to "alienate" itself. In this case, any opposition only *reinforces* the dominant discourse, which is a very effective way of understanding the equivalence between hegemony and universality. Not that the universal isn't "situated," nor that it lacks *real exteriority*; but this exteriority remains *inaccessible* to the dominated discourse (just as the thing-in-itself is inaccessible to Kantian consciousness) *as if* there were no real alterity. On the other hand, we can reverse the interpretation and hold instead that what universalizes a given worldview is precisely the necessity to incorporate resistances, oppositions, and objections.

We can go a step further by suggesting that it is the negative element secretly at work within dominant ideology, reflecting the irreducible presence of dominant ideology's other (its "ironic" element, as Hegel says with regard to *Antigone* and the Greek city or to *Rameau's Nephew* and bourgeois morality—*femininity* and *madness* serving as allegories of resistance), that provokes a discourse that has the universal power to fashion our experience of the world beyond the *limited* consciousness of its inventors and speakers. Here we arrive at the hypothesis that what makes an ideology dominant is the generalization of values and opinions not of the "dominant" but of the "dominated." The conclusion is by no means easy to admit, but it is an idea that haunts the Master-Slave dialectic, without which Marxian (or post-Marxian) discussions about the universalist character of bourgeois ideology would make no sense, especially when it comes to the persistent ambiguity of the notion of *human rights*. It has long been argued that the *universality* of human rights derives not only from their proclamation but also from the fact that every resistance and objection to the dominant order (let us call it capitalism or liberalism) gain legitimacy only insofar as they are themselves formulated in terms of a demand for or an extension of abstract "human rights." But one can just as reasonably argue that the dominant ideology essentially invokes "human rights" (or humanism, generally agreed to be the typical form of secular universalism in the moral, legal, and political spheres) because that is the general language in which insurrections and emancipatory struggles seek freedom and equality and challenge the order of established privileges. This would mean that the key to understanding universality as hegemony lies in the quasi-Lacanian trope: "The dominant receive their language/consciousness from the dominated in an inverted form." This is indeed an interesting way to reestablish the paradox of the enunciation *sub specie universitatis*: The "place" where the universal is situated as discourse, the place that particularizes the universal, is never immediately "its" place but can only be the place of its internal other, the place where its internal other *shall be*.[14]

STRATEGIES OF TRANSLATION

However decisive we consider these ambitious strategies of enunciation of the universal—the first based on the schema of Double Truth, the second on the conflictual relation between a sovereign Discourse and an internal Other—they still don't seem to exhaust the question. Given the many current debates about the heterogeneity of cultures, and given the possibilities created by the recognition of such heterogeneity as well as the obstacles it creates for an institution of the universal that is itself universal, it seems necessary to envision the paradoxes of its construction not only in terms of difference and conflict but also in terms of *translation*.

The debate (or perhaps we should say, *the new debate*) about the nature and effects of translation has now been going on for several decades, mainly in the field of "cultural studies." But no one doubts its philosophical dimension (which to a certain extent puts the orientations and future status of philosophy on the line).[15] Conceptions of translation informed by different philosophical backgrounds are also involved in the debates about universalism and communitarianism, or multiculturalism, which shows that the theories and concepts here take on immediate political significance. I would like to briefly describe how, in my view, another strategy for speaking the universal now comes into play (a divided strategy, to be sure, one whose intentions are directly challenged by its own development) and to address the traditional metaphysical question—of individuality and individuation—that this strategy will lead us to reconsider. Of course, the question will have to be considerably simplified.

Discussions about translation often begin by citing a paradox that has become a kind of commonplace—namely, that translation is *impossible* (or that it is an impossible *task*) even though it is performed every day on an enormous scale and is, therefore, *real*.[16] Such a starting point is necessary only as long as the ideal notion of translation on which it is based appears intrinsic to the activity of translation itself (as a norm, instrument, or obstacle). What is called impossible is a *perfect translation*, in which speakers or readers belonging to distinct linguistic universes (who use different languages to understand others and themselves or to read texts) would nonetheless attribute the same meanings (or even the same poetic values, the same images and affects) to different words and phrases. If most theorists agree that this type of correspondence (that is, this type of equivalence between languages) is never achieved in practice, except perhaps in extremely limited and completely artificial cases (where the term *language* only refers to a specialized code), we can still put it forward as an ideal type.

Such is clearly the case in W. V. Quine's famous doctrine of the "indeterminacy of radical translation" developed in his essay "Meaning and Translation"[17]: The initial thought experiment (a scene supposed to take place *prior to* any translation, during the "first meeting" between a missionary or ethnographer and a native, each ignorant of the other's language and with no mediator or interpreter present) demonstrates that the real processes of translation, if they occur (and there is no doubt that they occur), never provide the certainty that words refer to the same objects or that sentences convey the same meaning. Such a conviction can only result from shared learning processes, and—at a higher level, through what Quine calls a "semantic ascent"—as the result of different languages being used as different interpretations or nonisomorphic models of the same axiomatics. For Quine, languages are like "theories" that help speakers explain physical experiences: They can only be verified locally, or partially, and therefore have only *relative* truth. Needless to say, his analysis seeks to invalidate any positive concept of *semantic universality*, even one limited to the logico-scientific domain, and hinges on a more general critique of synonymy and meaning. Universality is the paradise lost of the human spirit.[18]

Only one other essay has perhaps exerted comparable influence on the contemporary philosophical debate about translation: Walter Benjamin's "The Task of the Translator."[19] This text obviously comes out of a completely different tradition (not logical but philological and hermeneutic, informed by the Romantic theories of language of Schlegel and Humboldt). It offers a nearly opposite view of translation (wherein translation doesn't seek to provide an equivalent to the expression of everyday experiences but to transpose poetic forms and aesthetic values from one written language into another).[20] Yet it seems to share a certain number of presuppositions with Quine's essay. Benjamin would consider the communication of information (*Mitteilung*), which for Quine is ultimately inaccessible, as quite feasible insofar as it bears only on "states of affairs," but as inessential to the art of translation. For what (literary) art truly seeks is to extend the aesthetic effect produced by a linguistic creation from its original language into another, which Benjamin describes as the development of a "seed" (*Samen*) or of a potential for dissemination always already given in (great) works of art. The efficacy of poetic writing derives not only from its ability to *transform* the original language whose expressive resources it exemplifies and completes, but also from its power to recreate other languages, by allowing itself to be transferred (*übertragen*) and translated (*übersetzen*). The "intention" thus manifested by translation is to attain a "pure language" (*eine reine Sprache*) in which there would exist, rather than an equivalence of codes, a complementarity, or better a "harmony" or "affinity" (*Verwandtschaft*), of expressive power. The idea of this language is one of community rather than substitutability—in other words, the *common fulfillment* of languages grounded in their irreducible diversity. Such fulfillment (which, although arising from purely historical practices, Benjamin aligns with the messianic end of history) nonetheless remains inaccessible; it functions as a "regulative idea" within each effort of translation.[21]

It is difficult to imagine two notions more distant from one another than a purely cognitive concept and a purely poetical concept of translation. And yet a common idea underlies Benjamin's and Quine's reasoning: that of a language that is initially (or that must initially be considered as) a *closed totality*, both in the sense that the language establishes an internal relationship between its elements and in the sense that it is associated with a *community of speakers* (and listeners, writers, and readers) who "belong" to it or to whom it belongs—whether the community is empirically constructed by the experiences of shared learning (in a behaviorist mode), and thus a product of convention, or is supposed to preexist as a "living" collective individual, carried along by its own dynamic of historical transformation and assigning individual subjects their horizons of meaning (in the Humboldtian tradition). To be sure, this common presupposition was also essentially accepted by nineteenth- and twentieth-century linguists (structuralists included), who made it the basis of their enumerations, typologies, and systematic analyses of languages: *Each language* or, along the same lines, each idiom, having received (but from whom? from itself, surely, but also from the *others* who "speak" it) its *particular name*—"French," "English," "Arabic," "Mandarin," or "Yiddish"—possessing its specific *grammatical rules*, its *words* or *expressions*, its *history*, etc., forms the *given totality* out of which the problem of translation arises.

There is no denying the validity of this way of representing things, with respect both to the transcendental (or quasi-transcendental) constitution of our experience (since the idea of a linguistic totality forming a community's symbolic bond implies the possibility of applying criteria of mutual understanding and misunderstanding, of recognition and nonrecognition, it makes drawing linguistic *boundaries* possible) and to institutional norms and practices (which don't only serve to exclude, for it is precisely these norms and practices that also make translation and "interpreting" essential practices in our societies). It would be ludicrous to claim that this idea has lost all relevance in our globalized "postmodern" world. But it is also impossible to ignore the great many facts concerning languages, translation, and cultures that highlight the *historical* nature of the linguistic-communitarian doublet or that contradict its dominant representation. I am not saying that these facts should remove all interest in Quine's and Benjamin's far-reaching philosophical problematics—on the contrary. But they can help us to establish the limits of their applicability and to change how we use such regulative ideas as "radical translation" or "pure language" so that they represent less the ideals toward which an enunciation of the universal as translation would desperately strive than the internal obstacles that it must struggle against.

To put things succinctly,[22] the historical character of the relationship between language as totality or system, on the one hand, and the community as the horizon of mutual understanding (or intercomprehension, recognition through dialogue), on the other, exemplifies the fact that the relationship is always a *political reality*, however abstract and general the idea that we place under this category. For several centuries (although never without exceptions or resistances), it has been associated with the dominant representation and institution of languages as national languages (or quasi-national, "ethnic," "civilizational") and with communities as peoples (present, past, or future), with or without a sovereign state. This relationship, understood as an absolute, ahistorical or transhistorical necessity, has tended to invert the actual relationship between translation and the normative character of national languages, obscuring the fact that many languages that have become "autonomous" entities are in fact the result of (institutional) translation practices (including scientific and literary translations as well as pedagogical, legal, commercial, etc., translations) and not the opposite. It has also tended to create the illusion that a process or effort of translation *begins with a constituted language* (even if translation completes or transforms it). We should instead recognize that situations in which speakers would "encounter" a totally unknown idiom have not existed for a very long time, if they ever existed at all, and that the Benjaminian idea of an "affinity" in which languages would no longer be "strangers to one another" is in a sense an *accomplished fact*—except that, rather than a harmony, it is an accumulation of conflicts, if not an actual war pitting each language against all the others. We already live in a world of omnipresent, rival "good" and "bad," "authorized" or "unauthorized," translations, thus in a world where certain languages are constantly incorporated into others (in a way much akin to what Bakhtin called *heteroglossia*).[23] A world of incessant *transgressions of established linguistic boundaries* that simultaneously entail the naturalization of speakers and the denaturation of idioms.

Think of the contradictory "linguistic rules" and heterogeneous "communities" comprising what we call "English" today (to the great dismay, it must be said, of a certain number of people who speak and write this language). What distinguishes this world is obviously not the equality or full recognition of the Other, even if, as I have argued elsewhere, it cannot function without a certain form of antagonistic *reciprocity*.[24] What distinguishes it is incompleteness (or the retrenchment of what is considered "untranslatable" or "unworthy of being translated") and unilateralism: Certain languages translate or mistranslate others, imposing themselves as "languages of translation" but also developing by incorporating a multitude of translations, whereas others remain subaltern, translated or untranslated, depending on relations of power and knowledge. These power relations define the *historicity* of the network of translations through which languages and communities (and thus cultures) become associated in a political entity.

To speak the universal as translation therefore means not only to advocate for translation (or for translating more), it means to translate anew, differently, elsewhere, for other groups and other individuals, who will thereby gain access to the work of translation. And because translation practices have produced (and continue to produce) political communities, reflecting on the possible transformations of these practices is an eminently *metapolitical* task, a philosophical task (in the sense that it returns to the primary elements of politics, elements that enable us to grasp the alternatives, powers, possibilities, and constraints of politics). Allow me to add three final points by way of conclusion, each of which clearly deserves a much fuller development than I will be able to provide here.

First of all, there has been a tendency in recent years *to enlarge and shift* the use of the category of "translation," especially in work by authors associated with "postcolonial" studies (such as Edward Said, Homi Bhabha, Gayatri Spivak, and Naoki Sakai),[25] who have moved from the idea of *translating languages* (or texts in a given language) to the idea of *translating "cultures."*[26] In a sense, this simply represents a new episode in the history of translations of the idea of translation—after the philology and semantics of Western modernity had confined translation to the construction of dictionaries and grammars, to the creation of parallel libraries, and more recently to the dubbing of film soundtracks—and once again testifies to the widespread circulation of information and cultural production between heterogeneous communities of meaning. But it also represents the recognition of the fact that the linguistic inequalities that inhibit communication and the sharing of languages are rooted in the collective history of the speakers who enter the public sphere with their traditions and sensibilities, their assigned places and statuses: They are no longer perceived solely as *speaking* subjects but also as *spoken* (and *written*) subjects. As we know, this does not necessarily mean emphasizing the fixed and exclusive nature of the traditional cultures that demand their political rehabilitation. Rather, the authors in question connect the activity of generalized translation with experiences of resistance, hybridity, split identity, textual dissemination, and the performative reversals of names and phrases. In my opinion, all this only makes sense if "cultures" are themselves conceived of as open evolving systems *of phrases, texts, discourses,* and *dialogues,* rather than as monadic "worldviews," and if the task of the multiple translators (who are always more numerous than certified translators, but fewer in number than they ought to be) is perceived as a contradiction in action, an active contradiction linked to the emergence of *evanescent mediators* who manage to "belong" simultaneously to different cultures and who therefore belong entirely to none, as something like "strangers from within."[27]

Second, the pragmatic categories that seem the most relevant for describing the experiences of generalized translation are not only those of speech acts—illocutionary force, use and intention, authority and context, etc.—which Lecercle discusses in the book I cited above, but are also those of *incomprehension* and *differend,* which turn the "impossibility of translation" into its paradoxical condition of possibility. Zygmunt Bauman, for example, uses the idea of "incomprehension," which he considers the *primary experience* that occurs *within* and *between* "communities of meaning," to *define universality as the result* of an activity of translation (rooted in everyday life) through which the bearers of differences learn "'how to go on'—to cope with the task of sorting out right, adequate or passable responses to each other's moves."[28] In a more tragic register, but against the same Wittgensteinian backdrop, Jean-François Lyotard describes phrase regimens that are incompatible or "incommensurable," because a wrong expressed or argued in one of these regimens can only be judged or evaluated in another, and more generally because they are not subject to a preexisting law. This does not mean that the universal rule cannot ever exist but that it can only exist if it is invented *after the event* in a singular way: to express the "impossibility of translating/translation" or *to juxtapose incompatible phrases in the same discourse,* "linking" them instead of masking them, returning from within referential language to the original that resists translation in order to expose their *differend*—that is the "move" (in the sense of "making a move" in checkers, chess, or a game of go) that defers untranslatability or shifts its *given* limits.[29] Here again, an element of universality "to come" (as Derrida would say) is in practice involved. And in both cases, violence and reciprocity come into play, even if the balance between them is bound to remain uncertain.

Lastly, it seems to me that we can indicate the type of metaphysical problems at stake in the project of generalizing and radicalizing the question of translation. They concern the construction of individuals. When the institutional, naturalized (not to say fetishized) correspondences between idioms and communities weaken and become conflictual, each of the two poles obviously being made up of "phrases" that do not spontaneously coincide, whose circularity must be "activated" by traditions and institutions (which implies that voices must be silenced and resistance suppressed), individuals are not freed from their transindividual relationships, emerging naked as if in a "state of nature." Rather, to borrow again from Quine's terminology, we see a different form of radical indeterminacy appear, a form that has less to do with the reference to *objects*, however, than with the reference to *subjects* (or their self-reference). This corroborates our contemporary experience of the limits of comprehension, wherein normal (in fact mythical) hierarchies of inclusion and exclusion are reversed. For example, it is much easier for me to have a discussion with an American colleague in a mixture of international English and academic French or Spanish than with a youth from the Parisian suburbs, whose words—not to mention peculiar slang—grammatical patterns, and pronunciation I don't completely understand, for they belong to a "nonstandard" variety of French, perhaps mixed with Arabic or Wolof (I had fewer difficulties with the working class of the older generation, or some of it at least, because my twenty years in the Communist Party had taught me the code and practice of a *convention* and even of a shared *institution*). Which "languages" are *identical*, which (and whose) are *different*? What practical realities do the official *name designations* of a language conceal? Where does the process of "translation" take place most: Is it within or across official linguistic boundaries? What is true of class with respect to language and national community, between which recent history seems to push us to reverse the balance of power, also holds for other disarticulations of social identities that traverse anthropological differences and cultural boundaries. In any case, the ontological correlate of a world of generalized translations is neither the emergence of a pure individual nor the individual's permanent suppression in the name of traditional communities that would assert their universal hold over communication and establish themselves as the absolute authority in matters of translation (although we are obviously not completely safe from such a development). Instead, it is a *problematic individuality*—that is, a suspended process of individuation and construction of the individual as a "capacity to evolve," to move, within a *universum* transformed into (as Ernst Bloch says) a *multiversum* that is subject to the contradictory tendencies of increasing standardization and the claim to differences, of identification with traditions and resistance to normalization.[30] On what should we base the singularity of the individual, and how do we gauge the possibility for an individual to free her or himself from the collective conditions of existence? That is indeed the problem common to all strategies of enunciation *sub specie universitatis.*

I have no illusions about the perfect consistency of my reflections. Obviously, I see several ways of organizing the various strategies I have just presented: *formally*, by relating them to different "grammatical models" (for example, disjunction, inclusion, consecution), or *historically*, by relating them to "stages" of our own philosophical culture ("premodern" or classical, "modern," and "postmodern," if you will)—in any case, the two approaches aren't incompatible. What prevents me from going too far in either direction is not only that I am not at all certain that they would allow a complete enumeration (in fact, I have simply taken them from certain aspects of my own theoretical work), it is also because I can already see why they aren't completely independent, neither conceptually nor politically. Nonetheless, I continue to believe that they are not easily subsumed under the single concept of the universal or of the language of the universal. In other words, they present us with intellectual *choices* that, it seems to me, will deeply divide philosophers. I offer them as working tools for posing from within philosophy the paradoxical question of its unknown future. But I offer them, too, in order to try to reflect on the possibilities of transforming *universitas*, this time understood as *university*, and, more generally, of transforming the educational systems "invented" by the West—assuming, that is, that these possibilities don't ultimately boil down to the alternative (a grim one, to be sure) between the status quo and the university's demise.

4

ON UNIVERSALISM

In Dialogue with Alain Badiou

I welcome the opportunity afforded me to publicly exchange words, ideas, and perhaps arguments with Alain Badiou on the theme of universalism and universality.[1] This is not the first time we have done so over the course of a long intellectual companionship, and perhaps, in a way, this topic has always been our common object—therefore also our point of heresy. But we each continue working and are led to highlight new aspects of the theme depending on the circumstances.[2]

I am firmly convinced that a philosophical discourse on the categories of the universal, universality, and universalism—their meaning and use—must be a critical discourse. That is to say, not simply a historical discourse, which would draw up an inventory and describe the context of discourses of the universal, certain of which themselves claim to be universalist, nor, of course, a discourse that would merely espouse one over others or try to expand an already very long list of discourses. In this respect, we (or some of us) have become cautious, perhaps even skeptical, because we have learned that the gap between theory and practice, principles and consequences, cognitive utterances and performative utterances, is inherent in the language of universalism and, to put things more generally, in all language that endeavors to "speak the universal," as our own discourses do this evening.[3] This equivocity takes multiple forms, but most particularly the form of universalist statements that hold different meanings and produce different effects depending on the time and place they are made, on the persons by whom and to whom they are made, or the form of universalist discourses that legitimize or institutionalize exclusions and, worse still, of universalist discourses whose categories are *based on exclusion*—in other words, on the negation of alterity or difference—but occasionally, too, inversely, the form of particularist or differentialist discourses that provide the paradoxical basis for inventing and determining the content of new, expanded forms of universalism. It seems—and I am stilling waiting for evidence to the contrary—that universalism *never does exactly what it says, nor says exactly what it does*. Consequently, the philosopher's task (the philosopher today, at *the present moment*) with respect to universalism is precisely to understand the logic of these contradictions and, in a dialectical way, to examine their dominant or subordinate aspects in order to discover how they function, how they are shifted or distorted in the interaction between theory and practice or, if you like, between discourse and politics. What I am excluding, therefore—already a gesture of exclusion, perhaps of the exclusion of the exclusive—is *a plea for or against universalism as such* or any one of its historical names.

I hope, however, that this type of critical attitude, which I would very much like to push toward a form of negative dialectics—despite previous uses of the term—all of whose effects I myself certainly cannot foresee, will not be misunderstood here. It is not that I have become hesitant or uncertain in my commitment to certain forms of secularism, to its names and key concepts, such as laicity, civil rights, democracy, egalitarianism, internationalism, social justice, etc. But I certainly don't think it would be sufficient or even wise to go out into the street or enter a lecture hall declaring, "I'm for laicity" (and thus against religious or cultural communitarianism), "I'm for internationalism" (and thus against all forms of national allegiance, which I have written about elsewhere as not actually being distinguishable from nationalism, which itself isn't without universalist aspects), etc.[4] In any case, I wouldn't want to do it without immediately asking questions like: "Which laicity?" "Which democracy?" "Which internationalism and nationalism?" etc. And also: "What for? Under which conditions?" As our teacher Althusser, who was certainly no relativist, used to say, "Everything depends on the conditions." And it is because I would like to incorporate certain of these conditions (including *negative conditions* or "conditions of impossibility") *into* the discourse of universalism or, to put it in more philosophical terms, because I would like to elucidate a discourse of universalism that allows us to incorporate its contradictory conditions, the contradictions that always already affect its conditions, that I am adopting a critical *and* dialectical point of view.

After these preliminaries, allow me now to indicate the three orientations that strike me as particularly significant from this point of view: The first has to do with the *dilemmas* or dichotomized utterances of universalism in philosophy; the second concerns the intrinsic ambivalence of the *institution* of the universal, or the universal as "truth"; and the third deals with what I would like to call, in quasi-Weberian terms, the *responsibility* (or responsibilities) involved in a politics of the universal that many of us support.

I will start by saying a few words about the dilemmas and dichotomies that, from the beginning, have informed our disputes over universalism. It is indeed intriguing as well as revealing that most of these disputes combine logical distinctions with ethical or political choices in order to construct symmetries, pairs of *notions, opposite conceptions* or *realizations* of universalism. One is tempted to say that in fact the content of the opposition always remains the same, at least in the modern era, but each time ends up reformulated according to the specific context. Yet this is not really satisfactory insofar as the question of conditions remains unaddressed. A dialectical approach, modeled on that followed by Hegel in his phenomenology of conflicting universalities,[5] would endeavor to describe these dilemmas in their own terms, to take them seriously, in order, each time, to discover what is at stake in their opposition. From there, it would also explain why debates about the opposition between the universal and the particular, and a fortiori between universalism and particularism, are much less interesting and decisive than debates opposing different conceptions of the universal or different universalities. Or, rather, it would explain why in reality the former merely conceal the strategic defense of a conception of the universal as the "negation" of its opposite, presented as the particular.

I am especially sensitive to this first approach because, some years ago, I myself forged a distinction between *intensive* universalism and *extensive* universalism.[6] I was interested in the figure of the citizen and in the history of the institution of citizenship, with its effects of exclusion and inclusion. In the modern era, citizenship has been closely associated, almost identified, with nationality. I explained that nationalism (*republican* nationalism, in any case)—but also other forms of universalism, such as the major religious discourses of redemption, which aim to suppress or neutralize natural and social differences—move in two directions: one seeking to establish equality or suppress distinctions, whether in real or symbolic terms, within a large or small community based specifically on this homogenization; the other tending to suppress every preestablished limit or boundary as part of the recognition and implementation of these principles, with the final goal of creating a cosmopolitical order that could be achieved either along revolutionary lines, *from below*, so to speak, or along imperialistic lines, *from above*. And I emphasized that these two orientations, while radically opposed and, indeed, incompatible, could both claim to exemplify the logic of universality or, better perhaps, of universalization. At around the same time, in 1989, Michael Walzer delivered his Tanner Lectures on the theme of "Nation and Universe," the first part of which was entitled "Two Kinds of Universalism." In it, he compares—with a distinct preference for the second term—"covering-law universalism," which brings together all claims to rights under one and the same law, all experiences of emancipation under the same narrative, and what he calls "reiterative universalism," whose immanent principle is differentiation or, rather, the virtual capacity of moral values and definitions of right to contest and communicate with one another in a process of mutual recognition.[7] Between these two dichotomies, between my *intensive-extensive* opposition and Walzer's *covering-reiterative* opposition, there were at once obvious affinities and striking divergences— the full import of which would be evident were I able to take up the concrete points of the debate here, such as the question of nationalism or messianism. But since we lack the time, allow me simply to point out, in a rather formal way, that such dichotomies, at once symmetrical and asymmetrical, or, if you prefer, descriptive and normative, become inevitable as soon as we actually engage in debates about universalism. They are a good sign that every speaker (and every discourse) of the universal is located *within* and not *outside* the field of discourses and ideologies that she or he wishes to explore.

It can't be by accident that many discourses on universalism and on the universal itself, perhaps even most of them, take a refutative form—what the Greeks called *elenchus*—which says not so much *what* the universal *is* as *what it is not* or *not only*. Indeed, no metalanguage of universality exists— in other words, the surest way to undermine the universality of a universalist discourse, as Hegel already knew, is to claim that it provides this metalanguage. But there are possibilities for displacement, for strategic choice, among the categories that give a specific explanatory or injunctive value to the distinction between antithetical forms of universalism. To classify these categories and to show how they can be at once very old and periodically renewed would involve sketching a speculative history of universality and universalities, a task that is tempting to undertake, since it would enable us to clarify certain contemporary debates.

For example, there is the opposition between *true* and *false universality*. A good recent illustration of this is provided by Alain Badiou himself. At the beginning of his essay on Saint Paul, Badiou contrasts a true humanism of equality, which erases or suppresses genealogical, anthropological, or social differences (Jewish/Greek, man/woman, master/slave), a universalism proceeding from Christianity and later secularized by modern republicanism, with a *false universalism*, a "simulacrum" of universalism (although certain problems may result from the fact that this simulacrum is in a sense much more real, or more effective, than its "true" counterpart)— namely, the universalism of the liberal world market (or perhaps the liberal representation of the world market), which is based not on *equality* but on *equivalence* and thus incorporates into its formal homogeneity the permanent reproduction of rival identities.[8] This second term pushes to the extreme the notion of "extensive universalism," making it an ontological product of *extension* or (de)territorialization as such. It has numerous philosophical antecedents, among which I would like to recall Rousseau's distinction between the "general will" and the "will of all," with which Badiou is quite familiar.[9] It would certainly have been challenged by Marx, who spent a good part of his intellectual life showing that the universality of the market is not only "real" but also "true"—that is, that it provides an ontological basis for the legal, moral, and political representation of equality—or by Foucault, who makes the market a fundamental form of "veridiction." We can also note with interest that another influential contribution to the current debate about universalism—I am thinking of Dipesh Chakrabarty's work, *Provincializing Europe: Postcolonial Thought and Historical Difference*[10]— also describes what the author calls equivalence or commensurability, terms associated with the "metanarratives" of value (or labor-value) and progress, as a dominant form of universalism, the result of which ultimately contradicts its egalitarian claims. From this, he draws the opposite conclusions. In Chakrabarty's terminology, translation is a generic term for universality, which leads him to compare "two models of translation."

Relying heavily on a certain Romantic conception of the uniqueness of languages and cultures, he opposes the principle of equivalence with a model that is also a form of universalism or translation, but a form based on the recognition of the untranslatable, and which he describes as heterogeneous, "nonmodern" (rather than postmodern) and "antisociological."

More than the antithesis of true and false, the old categories of the One and the Multiple here take center stage, such that we might speak of a *universalism of the One* (or of unity) and a *universalism of the Multiple* (or of multiplicity), the essential characteristic of multiplicity thus being *to exceed every possibility of subsumption* and therefore of common denomination, or exclusively in the form of a "negative denomination." [Badiou's project in *Being and Event* is founded explicitly on the possibility of substituting *multiplicity* for *unity* as the ontologically primary category, which, following a line of thinking close to Neoplatonism but identified above all with Mallarmé's metaphysics, leads him to conceive as an "ultra-one" the type of truth that creates an "event" by separating itself from being.]

This is part of a long story that goes back to the conflict between polytheistic and monotheistic religions in the ancient Hellenic-Semitic world but that still dominates the antitheses of the modern Enlightenment, as exemplified in the "war of universals" that opposed, on the one hand, the disciples of Kant and his univocal (in fact monotheistic) concept of the universality of the categorical imperative, and, on the other, the partisans of Herder, with his simultaneously historicist and polytheistic concept of the history of the world, in which unity exists only as the absent cause of the harmonious multiplicity of cultures. Now, as I said before, such antitheses can be shifted theoretically and practically, which we can demonstrate here albeit only in a very schematic way. Indeed, both Kant and Herder were typical champions of cosmopolitanism, together embodying the two versions that have continued to dominate uses of the notion to this day.

But let us take the example of a more recent discussion such as the one between Derrida and Habermas.[11] In a profound sense, they are both Kantians, and both refer to the Kantian definition of "cosmopolitical right," although we could say that their dispute retrospectively highlights a rift within Kant's discourse itself, exemplified by the distance between his book on *Religion within the Bounds of Bare Reason* (1793) and his *Doctrine of Right* (1797). Habermas would define cosmopolitanism as the limit or horizon of a line of progress that (whatever the obstacles and resistances encountered) tends to replace international relations with a "global domestic policy" (*Weltinnenpolitik*)—that is, not so much global institutional integration as an institutional exclusion of exclusion. Derrida, for his part, would allow the cosmopolitical motto provided that it is combined, through such notions as "hospitality" and "justice" (more precisely, "unconditional," not to say "categorical," hospitality and justice), with a radical critique of the legal foundations of politics. This did not prevent the two philosophers from joining forces after 9/11, not only *against* a certain form of sovereign unilateralism and the spread of a martial conception of politics, but also *for* the construction of a global transnational and transcultural public sphere, in what I will venture to call a "politics of the universal." Old Spinoza would perhaps have seen here an illustration of his idea, developed in the *Theologico-Political Treatise*, that in certain circumstances and under certain conditions, opposite theoretical *premises* or antagonistic conceptions of the universal can in practice lead to the same *consequences*. Of course, the reverse is also true.

I would now like to say a word about another aspect of the dialectic of universality that has interested me in the past and again more recently. It has to do with the *institution* of the universal, or with the institution of the universal as *truth*, which involves the added difficulty that the universal can no longer be contradicted except *from the inside*—that is, on the basis of its own logic or premises. Not because the universal would be imposed by some authority *prohibiting* contradiction or refutation but because the contradiction is already contained in the definition of the universal itself. As we shall see, this situation is closely connected to the fact that certain forms of universality derive their power not from the absolute authority of the institutions in which they are embodied, but rather from their capacity to be continuously challenged on the basis of their own principles or discourses.

These types of discussions are pointless or incomprehensible unless we turn, at least allusively, to a concrete case, although I admit that the one I am thinking of is both ideologically determined and politically tendentious—perhaps what I have to say here applies solely to this specific case. That may mean that the history of universality is composed only of singularities. The singular universality in which I am interested is not the Pauline affirmation of the equality of the faithful, later transferred to all of humankind, which, in Alain Badiou's view, is the prototype for a charismatic foundation of universalism.[12] It is something quite different: the civic principle or proposition of "equal liberty" (which I have suggested be read as a single word: equaliberty). In English, the formula appears in certain "tracts" from the seventeenth-century English Levellers, which indicates the close connection uniting it to the ideals of what is conventionally called the "bourgeois revolution."[13] But its philological roots extend to a much older tradition, to the legal and moral philosophy of the Romans (who practically identify *aequum ius* with *aequa libertas*) as well as, in perhaps a more significant way (although this point raises translation problems for terms like *isonomia* and *parrhēsia*), to the democratic ideals and discourses of the Greek *polis*. It will go on to generate continual effects, *reiterated* up to the present day in the discourses of democratic institutions and social movements of liberals and socialists alike. I will leave all this aside because it would indeed make for a very long story. Let us merely recall the twin formulations of the American and French Declarations of 1776 and 1789, which by themselves represent an interesting *iteration* from within the original event and inscribe the bond of reciprocity constitutive of *equality* and *freedom* (or *independence*) in partially convergent and partially divergent contexts. Although my understanding of the *act* of this proposition follows in large measure from what Hannah Arendt says about its significance for the institution of the political, I would not say, as she does, that we have, in one instance, a "revolution (or a constitution) of freedom" and, in the other, a revolution of equality (or "happiness") (*On Revolution*). In both, we have instead a strong and absolute expression of the necessary link between the concepts of freedom and equality, with, however, a permanent tension between them that reveals their impossible equilibrium. From my previous discussions of this expression,[14] I will mention three ideas here.

(1) The first concerns the *refutative structure* of the proposition or, if you prefer, its realization within an *elenchus*, a "negation of negation." In constitutional texts, this proposition appears in a positive form, affirming that "men are born free and equal" or are such by nature, by birthright, etc. In other words, only institutional violence can deprive them of these rights. But such formulas spring from revolutions or insurrections, in the broad sense, and they encapsulate their effect. They are based on the theoretical critique and the practical rejection of established inequalities or privileges. More specifically, they are based on the conviction—to my mind, totally vindicated by history—that discrimination goes hand in hand with subjection

(what is traditionally called *tyranny*), and vice versa, that subjection and tyranny go hand in hand with discrimination and inequalities. Consequently, political institutions, *citizenship*, if you will, must be founded on a *double rejection* of tyranny and privileges and not on a single, or rather unilateral, rejection. More profoundly, political institutions embody the *negative link* between the two core values of citizenship. This has been demonstrated many times in the history of emancipatory movements, and particularly in the labor movement, the feminist movement, and anticolonial struggles. I would like to connect this logical negation with a crucial political fact concerning the power and effectiveness of this form of universalism: Real states or societies, including those we call democratic, are composed of inequalities and authoritarian relationships. But far from its practical failures and limitations destroying the democratic principle, the practical contradiction itself reveals the reason for the principle's durability. Individuals and groups that are subjected to or victims of discrimination rebel in the name or in defense of principles that are recognized officially and denied in practice. It is the possibility of rebellion inscribed in their very principle, when the principle "has gripped the masses," as Marx puts it, that accounts for democracies' capacity to survive, be it at the risk of conflicts or civil wars.

(2) I would now like to recall a second idea: Although it must (always again) be instituted, equaliberty is not simply one institution among others. We might say that in modern democracies it represents the *archi-institution*, the institution that precedes and conditions all the others. It is in this context that Hannah Arendt's profound reflection on "the right to have rights" assumes its full significance—and it is no accident that it appears within the framework of her analysis of the most extreme forms of totalitarian destruction of human life, those rooted in the negation of the individual rights instituted by universalist nation-states.[15] Equaliberty therefore refers to the preeminent right to have rights but it emphasizes the active side of the notion. In practice, this means that a right to rights can exist only in contexts where individuals and groups *do not receive them* from an external sovereign power or transcendent revelation but instead *confer this right upon themselves* or *grant themselves rights reciprocally*. It would be worthwhile to develop this idea of a limit-institution, or of an institution of the institution itself, in order to address its gradual transition from a classical naturalistic form of discourse on human rights (men, or humans, are *free*

and equal by nature) to a modern historical form, in which universality is grounded in the *contingency of insurrection*, or, if you prefer, of struggle, rather than in essence. It would also be worthwhile to link this limit situation, which essentially appears in the form and context of the negation, to the contradictions that eventually affect every *positive institution* of equaliberty or democracy. The entire modern history of democratic regimes and struggles attests to the difficulty—the internal obstacle—that hinders *real institutions*, or real political regimes, from advancing both toward equality and toward freedom, or of protecting one from the other. There is hardly a single case where we see the two principles realized simultaneously, or if they are, then merely as a tendency, an exigency. From this I conclude not that civic universality is an absurd myth, but on the contrary that it exists as an *effort*, a *conatus*. The mainspring of this tendency remains the force of the negative, magnificently expressed in certain philosophical formulas like "the part of those who have no part" ["*la part des sans-parts*"], in Jacques Rancière's work, and "the power of the powerless" ["*le pouvoir des sanspouvoir*"], in Merleau-Ponty's.[16]

(3) Finally, I would like to return to a third idea, perhaps the most troublesome of all, but one without which every discourse on universalism is, in my opinion, futile: It concerns the *violence* inherent in the institution of the universal. I stress that this violence is intrinsic and not additional, not something that we could blame on the ill will, weakness, or constraints weighing on the bearers of the universalist institution, because it is the institution itself, or its historical movement, that designates them as its bearers. I said when I began that neither the gap between theory and practice, especially when it comes to realizing the former in a historical and political form, nor the perverse effects of exclusions caused by the very principles of inclusion are mere accidents. We can't simply say: Let's just give it another try, this time everything will work out and we will avoid the dark side of universality. The intrinsic violence of the universal, which is among its conditions of possibility, is also among its conditions of *impossibility* or self-destruction—it is a "quasi transcendental," as Derrida would say. The dark side thus belongs to the dialectic itself; it belongs to the *politics of the universal* (an expression that, unlike certain contemporary authors like Charles Taylor, I do not identify with a *politics of universality*, as opposed to a "politics of difference," because a politics of difference is *also* logically a politics of the universal).[17]

The violent exclusion inherent in the institution or in the realization of the universal can take numerous forms, which are not equivalent and do not call for the same politics. A sociological or anthropological approach would emphasize that opposing discrimination and modes of subjection through a civic universality expressed in legal, educational, and moral forms entails that we define *models of humanity* or *social norms*. Foucault and others have drawn our attention to the fact that the Human excludes the nonhuman or inhuman, that the Social excludes the "nonsocial" or "asocial." These are forms of *internal exclusion* that affect intensive universalism, as I have called it, more than extensive universalism. They do not have to do with territory or *imperium*, but rather with the fact that the universality of citizens, of citizens as human subjects, is indexed to a community that claims to be homogenous, or endowed with a specific and normative "collective identity." But a political and ethical approach, which we can connect with the idea or formula of a "community without community"—or without an *already existing* community—must envision still another form of violence intrinsically tied to universality: the violence perpetrated by its representatives and supporters against its adversaries, in particular its internal adversaries—that is, potentially any "heretic" within the revolutionary movement. Many philosophers—whether or not they are themselves adversaries or instead fervent advocates of universalist programs and discourses, such as Hegel in his chapter on the Terror in the *Phenomenology* or, inversely, Sartre in his *Critique of Dialectical Reason* with respect to "fraternity-terror"—have emphasized this relation, which is clearly bound up with the fact that certain forms of universalism embody the logical characteristic of "truth"—in other words, they suffer no exception. Badiou himself has referred to this in certain of his political writings, revealing himself to be closer to Sartre than to Hegel on the point. If we had the time (or perhaps later in the discussion), we would have to examine the consequences that follow from such a position. I spoke earlier about a "quasi-Weberian" conception of responsibility, obviously thinking of the famous lecture on *Politik als Beruf* in 1919.[18] Responsibility, in this case, would not merely oppose "conviction" (*Gesinnung*) but, more generally, the ideals themselves, or the ideologies that include a universalist principle and objective. In this regard, a politics of human rights is typically a politics that aims to institutionalize a universalist ideology, and prior to that: to ideologize the principle that disturbs and defies existing ideologies. Universalist ideologies are not the only ones that can become absolutes, but they are certainly the ones whose realization implies the possibility of radical intolerance and internal violence. This is not a risk that we should avoid, for it is, in fact, inevitable. But it is a risk that must be recognized, and that charges the representatives, spokespeople, and agents of universalism—among whom Badiou and myself, as philosophers and perhaps as unrepentant "communists"—with a responsibility that, in the end, is no small thing.

5

A NEW QUARREL

In the new "quarrel of universals" that now occupies philosophy and other overlapping disciplines, a quarrel supplanting the "quarrel of humanism" that once divided philosophers into apparently irreconcilable camps in the 1960s and 1970s, thus revealing some of the stakes involved in the previous debates, the question today is not only whether one is *for* or *against* the universal; the question is also *how one defines* the universal—a term whose surprising equivocity has become increasingly clear.[1] Still more fundamentally, the question is how one should articulate the relationship between three related but heterogeneous terms whose widespread use has prompted conflicting claims: *the universal* (if it is indeed singular), *universality* (which immediately calls for clarification and determination, for there is no universality "in itself," not even "the universality of the universal"), and *universalisms* (which, decidedly plural, are thrown straightaway into a kind of "performative contradiction").

I am not going to address these questions "scholastically," by way of a systematic division of the subject matter, but rather by way of a *conceptual narrative* in which I intend to follow the common thread of my own *encounters* with certain reversals of the presuppositions of traditional philosophy. Some of these reversals are part of a long history (whose procedures have been partially noted or summarized in the foregoing essays); others, on the contrary, were surprises that awaited me in my use of certain categorical combinations (such as "equaliberty" and "co-citizenship"), or in the use that others chose to make of them, often without my knowledge. By drawing on these encounters and by putting them to work, however, I am not primarily looking to verify or reappropriate but rather to let myself be guided by those trajectories along which I hadn't in fact imagined my arguments were likely to lead. This is why, in line with what to my mind constitutes one of the implications of philosophical "method," I am aiming not so much to conclude as to *unfinish*, as actively as possible, the essays that I have already written.

I will proceed in three parts, the second of which will serve as mediation and will itself be subdivided. In the first, I will situate the question of the universal and its variations within the field that seems to me to constitute, instead of the primary domain of philosophical work (for there is no "first philosophy"), the strategic site of intersecting domains: *philosophical anthropology*, understood as the analysis of the historical differences of the human and of the problem that those differences pose to their bearers. In my conclusion, I will return to what in a previous essay struck me as the latest of philosophy's strategies for articulating its "object" *sub specie universitatis*— namely, the strategy of *translation*, whose significance I seek to grasp by means of an expression that in my view remains partially enigmatic: *Les langues se parlent* [*languages are spoken/speak to one another*].[2] In the second part, I will lay out the difficulties that I believe can be identified in every philosophical and political usage of the universal and its "doubles" (universality and universalism) according to *three aporias*. The first is the aporia of the *multiplicity of the "world,"* or of the universe as *multiversum*; the second is that of *Allgemeinheit* or *All(en)gemeinheit*, in other words, the irreducible gap between the universal and the common (or community); and, finally, that of *co-citizenship*, the form of belonging to a political unity *to come*, a unity whose law of belonging (membership) would be the heterogeneity within equality or the political participation of those foreign to the community. I have named the aporias in this way in order to locate in each of them the question of anthropological differences while leaving open the possibility of the displacement of those differences within a problematic of generalized translation. I wouldn't say that these aporias "sum up" everything there is to know about the stakes of the quarrel of universals, but I would suggest that they allow us to give those stakes an intelligible *order* in light of our current priorities.

ANTHROPOLOGICAL DIFFERENCES
AND "HUMAN" SUBJECTIVITY

What I am calling "anthropological difference" does not refer to every kind of diversity that might be registered a posteriori or become an object of reflection within the field of the "human" or "human sciences." It refers to *certain specific differences*, which, I believe, serve in the *modern* era above all to "govern" people's humanity and their unequal access to citizenship. One common, if initially only formal, feature of these differences is that they are at once *indissoluble* and *unassignable*. In a previous essay, where I attempted to describe this *double bind* and to reflect upon its effects, I privileged three of these differences: the difference between the *normal* and the *pathological*, the division of humanity into *"races"* and *"cultures,"* and the difference between the *sexes*, a difference *overdetermined by that of sexualities.*[3] Without going into the details again here, I would like to return to what in my opinion justifies privileging these three differences and to review certain difficulties that arise as a result.

In my essay, I stated from the outset that this list of differences was *indicative*: sufficiently exact to cover subjective experiences and institutional mechanisms and to highlight historical transformations, but too approximate to avoid the immediate objection of being *incomplete* and *heterogeneous*. Moreover, in an earlier version of the essay (directly related to the question of *exclusions from "active" citizenship* during the revolutions of the late eighteenth century), I had in fact concentrated on *two* types of "differences"—the difference between the sexes and intellectual difference—the second of which would later provisionally disappear.[4] It isn't that I forgot about it (all the less so given that I remain convinced that it plays an increasing role in the reproduction of class divisions in an age of "cognitive capitalism" and the collapse of the great systems of public education). Rather, by confronting these three other differences, I believed I had found a way to isolate the one thing that belongs to all anthropological differences, despite their heterogeneity, and makes them the very object of those questions that subjects ask themselves with regard to their "humanity" in modern societies. Again, this common feature is the existence of a double bind that makes certain differences at once *indissoluble* and *undefinable* (especially in the form of a boundary or demarcation, even if every definition involves a process of demarcation). And in the same text, I just as quickly added: indissoluble and undefinable except through overt or covert *violence*, which is the everyday affair of the social institutions of difference. "Indissoluble" means that we *will never be able to think* that such differences do not empirically exist (even if attributing them to nature or culture always presents problems), or that they do not govern the organization of social relations.

A thought experiment in which we attempt to *eliminate differences* should prove convincing: To assert that no differences exist between the sexes, or between normal and pathological (physical and mental) states for a given individual in a given society or for a given way of life, or, for that matter, that no ethnic or cultural differences exist in humanity, seems at once patently absurd, contrary to the facts, and generative of the kind of violence theoretically prohibited in every civilization (which does not mean that that violence is not carried out in practice).[5] That we are unable to deny these differences means that we are unable to *confuse* the terms that they designate, terms whose differentiation structures real human experience and is central to a whole series of "fundamental" social institutions (for example, in education, the difference between childhood and adulthood). On the other hand, there is no less violence in *assigning* anthropological differences to "spaces," "classes," or "groups" of humans separated from one another, in other words, in *defining* them exclusively and in using that exclusion to establish individuals' unique *identity*. Such is true for the difference between the sexes—not, however, understood as the difference between "men" and "women" but as the difference between *the feminine "character"* and *the masculine "character,"* an imaginary polarity inscribed within the very structure of unconscious desire of which every subject, each in her or his own way, partakes, and that accounts for more or less complex "sexual orientations." Such is true for the difference between the normal and the pathological (perhaps the most obvious case because of the crucial work done over the last half century, prompted especially by Goffman and Foucault, on the notions of "health," "illness," "madness," "handicap," "delinquency," etc.), which no less remains a powerful instrument of segregation and exclusion, an instrument informed by the fantasy of a "subhumanity." Such is also true for the question of ethnic differences provided that we immediately stipulate that—I will come back to this—the competing "criteria" serving to identify human communities (in particular communities of hereditary or genealogical descent), whether "race" or "culture," are neither fixed nor independent of one another, and, above all, that *the difference* that plays a fundamental political role (in the modern bourgeois period, at any rate) is not a *first-level* difference (that separating Whites from Blacks, Europeans from Asians, the French from the Germans, or Christians from Muslims) but a *second-level* difference (that separating the "neutralization" of forms of belonging from their "absolutization"). It is precisely at this level that a double violence reveals itself: on the one hand, that of negating differences and, on the other, that of erecting them into a principle for the *confinement of individuals* to mutually exclusive identities.

The thesis that I advanced is that bourgeois society simultaneously *naturalizes* these differences (or, as Foucault puts it, "objectifies" them through knowledge elaborated in a scientific form and correlated with the power of certain institutions: prisons, schools, and hospitals, to which we should add borders, marriage, and so on) and uses them as a means to "verify" inequalities between citizens or simply to *exclude certain humans from citizenship*, as if this fundamentally arbitrary exclusion were part of the "natural order of things." To this end, bourgeois society exploits the fact that major anthropological differences are undeniable or indelible. But since these are at the same time unassignable and, ultimately, undefinable (except, that is, through the negation of their opposite), violence inevitably turns against the mechanisms of classification, hierarchization, and exclusion. This is by no means the least of the catalysts of the many *revolts* punctuating the entire history of bourgeois society, revolts in which "minorities" demand equal rights (and, more generally, social recognition) in the name of official principles whose advantages they have been denied. However—and this is the other side of the same double bind affecting not only the social order but also movements of resistance, insurrection, and emancipation—since violence lies *both* in the denegation of differences and in their absolutization, every revolt must face the difficulty of deciding whether it will emphasize the legitimacy of difference, the right to particularity, or the primacy of universality and the need for its reconfiguration on new grounds. In general, the difficulty can only be overcome "tactically," provisionally. The history of feminism or, more recently, of postcolonial immigrant movements for the recognition of their civil and cultural rights offers a telling example of the dilemma. All these contradictions are at the core of *modern universalism* such as it was established, beginning in the eighteenth century, on the basis of the market and nation-states, the latter of which are at the same time *states of law*, in which citizens are entitled to fundamental rights defined individually according to the great principles of freedom, equality, and self-ownership. The contradictions constitute the dialectical form of modern universalism, at least from the perspective of its *political history*.

But the question that increasingly arises today is whether the forms of this bourgeois rationality still allow us to make sense of the connection between the differences that characterize *humans as humans* and the institutions of the universal, or the forms of institutional universality. This uncertainty inevitably extends to our judgment of whether we actually consider valid the *universalist discourses* that "found" modern political constitutions and represent their symbolic *point of pride*—for example, the "cosmopolitanism" theorized by Enlightenment philosophers. To what extent do those who are the agents of the dialectic of social normalization and emancipatory revolt still view the dialectic within this framework? Essentially, the question is whether we are leaving modernity behind and, if so, *how*.

At this point, I would like to mention two related difficulties. The first brings us back to the meaning of the adjective "anthropological." The dominant thinking of the bourgeois period, and thus of our own education, is *humanist* and the social institutions in which its relations of power, dependency, exploitation, and communication have been configured are *human* institutions. "Human" should be understood in both senses here: as immanence, as opposed to the divine or supernatural order, and as exception, the exceptionality of human beings in the natural world (which obviously ignores the fact that human individuals can also be considered living beings among other living beings). This is why I have called anthropological differences those differences exclusively *between humans*. In doing so, it may appear that I have neglected another difference, which the Western philosophical tradition (in particular since Aristotle) has defined as twofold in that it separates the human considered in its unique "essence" both from *animality* and from divinity or the *divine*. This twofold difference is specific to *ontology*, although it also has anthropological significance. We might even say that it *founds* an *anthropologia perennis*, an integral part of the metaphysical tradition, which, instead of considering politically constituted differences as they exist within the "human species," *founds politics* on a definition of the species.[6] Yet what is striking when one examines this (grand) philosophical discourse is the fact that it imagines a hierarchy within which the human is located in a "medial" position between two varieties or two aspects of the *inhuman* (the divine and the animal). In a certain sense, the inhuman envelopes the "finitude" of the human from which the human simultaneously draws away. Now, the hierarchy is not linear, for the "boundaries" between humanity and animality, like those between humanity and divinity, form zones of contact inhabited by intermediary, subhuman, or superhuman figures (for Aristotle, there is the "natural" slave on one side and heroes or wise men on the other). One can then reverse the perspective and claim that in reality the human is a problematic essence in which elements of animality and divinity converge and conflict. The same claim also allows one to differentiate and hierarchize human types according to their degree of proximity to or distance from the inhuman.

This view of things has by no means disappeared from the system of differences envisioned by bourgeois universalism: there is still the tendency to deify (or to sublime, to endow with transcendence) the "superior" terms of a difference (the masculine with its innate "rationality," the normal or the "sane," "developed" races or cultures, the intellectual versus the manual or the affective) and, above all, to *animalize* the "inferior" terms (those subject to relegation or social exclusion: the feminine, the pathological, "primitive" cultures). Yet this entire normative structure is no doubt changing today. On the one hand, contemporary anthropological discourse has tended to reformulate ontological difference in terms of oppositions between humanity, animality, and the *machine* or technology. As Francis Wolff has rightly shown, the computer is now to man what the gods once were to the *anthropoi* of Greek philosophy.[7] On the other hand, the hierarchical schema no longer functions along a vertical axis, for animality is perceived as a dimension of "life," while life itself now stands in a relation of potential equivalence with the machine. This is why the human is defined less as a *middle term* (Aristotle) between its own higher and lower limits than as a "moment" or phase in the ongoing fusion of two manifestations of natural power—the living and the mechanical.[8]

I would like to turn now to a second difficulty. It concerns the idea of "ethnic" difference, or rather its name, which, the reader will no doubt have noticed, made me somewhat uneasy above. Now, in most current debates on universalism and its opposites or obstacles, this is the issue that comes to the fore, because it relates to the question of *communities* (one of whose fundamental types is often considered to be ethnicity), or to the antithesis between universalism and communitarianism. As I have already mentioned, the modality in which the difference between human groups becomes a problem does not depend on the *fact* of their existence. What is problematic, rather, is determining *the extent to which this diversity is "essential" to or constitutive of the human*. Once again, there is violence on both sides, whatever the criteria one applies (language, culture, kinship, or, shifting the question of collective diversity to another domain, the *religious diversity of the human species*). There is violence in the "standardizing" denegation of differences and in their relegation to "contingency," just as there is violence in the forcing of differences, a process that transforms them into immutable forms of belonging that individual identity merely serves to reflect. Now, what seems to me characteristic of the current situation is that the idea of ethnic diversity hasn't at all disappeared but rather has tended to lose the unifying *national* bases with which the history of the last five centuries provided it; these bases gradually extended from Europe to the rest of the planet (the famous *jus publicum Europaeum*), culminating in the "cosmopolitical" representation of humanity as a system of "united nations" sharing the same moral values and recognizing the same legal norms.[9] If such is the case, the current situation may very well reveal one way in which globalization, a *real universality*, has radically transformed the questions of difference and universalism.

This is why the idea of human diversity (one of the "regulative principles of reason," if Kant is to be believed) floats between several codes, each seeking to *intensify* the exclusiveness of differences: the heterogeneity of cultures, the "return of race," or, much the same thing, the normalization of racism encouraged by the indelible remains of colonial discrimination. Or, instead, the idea of human diversity disappears in the shadow of generalized hybridity, which gradually turns every group into the product of a blending of all the others. Between the imperialism of identity and the utopia of limitless hybridity, the ever-present double bind of anthropological difference thus reaches a kind of limit point. Yet it is precisely because of this that we must seek out a *critical* apparatus for thinking *the universality of differences* and the irreducible conflicts that that universality entails. This apparatus must take into account both the *subjective* and *institutional* aspects of the conflict inherent in the idea of the universal. In other words, it must not only scrutinize the way in which "universalist" institutions control, exploit, repress, recognize, or promote the differences that those institutions consider constitutive of humanity, but also the way in which subjects *perceive and think of themselves* as the site of conflict.

THE DESIRE TO KNOW

Starting from this modest sketch of the evolution (or current *dissemination*) of "ethnic difference," I will try to move closer to this objective, but by focusing on the *entire set* of differences with which I began. For it seems to me that what follows pertains to all differences given their constant interaction and overlapping (the intersection of race and sex no doubt being the most prominent example).[10] Not long ago, in a text where I brought the Freudian theme of infantile "sexual curiosity" into a discussion of race as the "interpellation" of individuals by their genealogical identity, I wrote that the notion of ethnic identity does not represent a "prejudice" but corresponds instead to a *desire to know* in human individuals that is constitutive of their being as subjects (and that is, of course, socially and historically conditioned while at the same time irreducible to mere ideological inculcation).[11] I believe that we can in fact extend the supposition to the entire problem of anthropological differences as matrices of subjectivity; we can posit that not only are anthropological differences *a problem* for every human being (a more or less conscious, more or less agonizing problem, a problem more or less "solved" by means of education, environmental factors, science, or religious belief), but also, at the same time, that *the human is the being for whom the different ways or possibilities of being human are a problem.* I would even go so far as to advance as a philosophical thesis that, in the idea of the human as such, there is essentially *nothing else* except for this insistent question regarding differences—whether one perceives them *in the other* (through the "relation" or the "nonrelation" that one establishes with others: How are others *different*? How are they *not different*?) or seeks out differences (and fears or desires them) in oneself.

The thesis is only apparently tautological. It is of course deliberate on my part that it somewhat echoes those formulations employed by Heidegger in *Sein und Zeit* (1927) that prefigure the thematic of "care" (*Dasein* is the being or existent for which the *mode of being* is in question or open to question). However, I am attempting to reintroduce, through the problem of difference, the anthropological dimension that Heidegger sought to eliminate.[12] It is possible that bourgeois modernity, in adopting the idea of anthropological differences according to the double bind that I described above—a modernity motivated by the necessity both of *codifying* differences socially and of subsuming them within a universalist ideal that "reduces" them to empirical differences—has ultimately intensified the question and made individual and collective consciousness expose its desire to know, just as Foucault describes in *The Will to Knowledge* (*The History of Sexuality*, vol. 1, 1976). But we also have to acknowledge that there is something transhistorical in the *very fact* of the desire to know when applied reflexively to the *multiplicity* that constitutes the human. According to Freud, human subjects are constantly, unconsciously, asking the "infantile" sexual question that they have inherited and will transmit (or transfer) to others: *Am I masculine or feminine* or both at the same time? Above all, *how*, in what way, am I one or the other or both? But these are the same subjects who, sooner or later, will ask themselves: Am I "normal," "healthy," "sick," "insane," or, perhaps, a "criminal" or "monster"? And what do such differentiations *mean* for oneself and others? What ethical or political implications do they have? Do they impart, to one's own judgment or to that of others, an objective value or only the value of an opinion or convention? And finally, of course, these are the same subjects who ask themselves what it is to be "foreign," even and especially if this legally codified demarcation has initially been presented as obvious, if the question has already been *resolved in advance* by the institutions that grant membership and assign identities (and sometimes withhold them). Obviously, the interesting thing is that such questions always concern both oneself and others, or rather they *circulate* between self and other, in an endless interplay of identifications and distantiations that constitute subjectivity. These questions are therefore also inherent in the experience of social relations and, especially, in the experience of relations of *power* and *domination*, the extreme form of which is exclusion or, indeed, elimination.

THREE APORIAS OF UNIVERSALITY

On this basis, I would now like to recall and reformulate the three aporias characteristic of the enunciation of the universal. Although I have had the opportunity to discuss them elsewhere, here I will focus on the manner in which they clarify the stakes of the anthropological problem. "Aporia" means that a *question* is posed in such a way that it cannot be ignored but in terms such that the only available answer is the infinite reiteration of the question itself. Naturally, this situation, which is frustrating from a positivist point of view, is also what prevents us from bringing the problem of universalism *to a close*. And that is precisely what is important.

The first aporia is that of the "*world*," or that of the representation of the function of differences in the world.[13] It underscores the fact that the construction of a concept of the universal and, consequently, the way in which a universalist discourse is formulated always have a *cosmological* dimension. This is because every reflection on identity and difference entails an attempt to organize or situate them in *places* determined to be "appropriate" (in the sense of *convenientia*, the term with which Latin authors, following Cicero, translated the Stoics' *oikeiôsis*, that is to say, the *propriety* of certain actions, certain roles, certain moral attitudes, to the order of the world of which they are a part).[14] Naturally, the concept of "world" changes profoundly in meaning over the course of history. Such is true as much for the "natural" world (or, alternatively, the universe) as for the "social" world (the system of social relations and the rights or duties that proceed from them), and likewise for its moral correlate, *cosmopolitanism*. Nonetheless, I think we can say that the desire for knowledge that concerns the relationship of subjects to the differences that make them *determined* humans is also a desire for knowledge and representation that concerns the system of *places in the world* and the existence of a place suitable to each person's anthropological difference (or differences). This is the place where one can *enter into relation* or meet with others in a constructive way (for example, in antiquity, the *oikos* or "household" was where a free adult male could enter into unequal but equitable relation with women, children, or slaves, whereas the public square, the *agora* from which the city was governed, was where he entered into contentious but equal relation with other free adult males). From this perspective, an enormous gulf exists between what we might schematically call the ancient model and the modern model. Within the former, all places are differentiated, even if certain are in a relationship of reciprocity, because differences are distributed according to "local" and "moral" *complementarities* that allow them to fulfill their natural function. It is only the *totality* or totalization of these differences, each considered in its place, that has a value of universality (and that, in philosophy, manifests a *logos*, an objective "reason"). On the other hand, in the modern model, configured by civilbourgeois universality through the "secularization" of monotheistic universalisms, each individual subject is directly, on her or his own account, the bearer of the universal (not only objectively, but subjectively, through self-consciousness). The result (which Kant made a moral criterion) is that subjects can come to occupy *the same place* or, better still, come to occupy the place of another (an other who, for each individual, is "completely other"—that is, any "other" at all). There must therefore ideally exist a universal place, which is simultaneously the place of the universal, insofar as subjects, as they come to occupy it, *are universalized*. One could also say that this is the place of *transcendental equality* among subjects, who must inhabit it and must become interchangeable to do so, but without losing their singularity. Naturally, universalist discourse constructs a "world" in which such a place not only exists but constitutes the center or mainspring of the social and political order. Thus, in the words of Althusser, who, if memory serves, attributed the pun to Tran Duc Thao: All transcendental *egos* are transcendental *equals*.[15]

There is, however, a significant consequence to the institution of cosmo-logical equality by means of the "transcendental" (that is, by means of the inscription in human nature of a moral *destination* transcending differences and oppositions)—namely, the emergence of what Michel Foucault, draw-ing on Kant in *The Order of Things* (1966), calls the "empirico-transcendental doublet": in other words, the fact that anthropological differences are rele-gated to the empirical realm of particularisms where they are supposed to belong to individuals in a way that is merely contingent and neutralizable or, "by law," simply nonexistent with respect to the essential characteristics of the *species*. Yet major anthropological differences (those that, at least in part, Kant examines and attempts to classify, depending heavily on psycho-pedagogical, masculine, Eurocentric, and nationalist stereotypes, in his *Anthropology from a Pragmatic Point of View* of 1798) do not have to do with individual particularities: They are *themselves universal*, despite consisting essentially of *unstable*, problematic divisions. This is why they inevitably reemerge within moral and legal universality, where they introduce in-equality and even exclusion (that is, they introduce *places* that are *withheld*, *removed*, from cosmopolitical humanity even though they are inherent in its construction or progress). Gayatri Spivak's work (*Critique of Postcolo-nial Reason*, 1999), in the US, along with that of Max Marcuzzi (on Kant's *Geography*) and Raphaël Lagier (on Kantian racial theory), in France, have convincingly shown that, in terms of culture, it is impossible to describe his-tory as a teleological process that fulfills the conditions of transcendental equality without at the same time registering within that history a differ-entiation between capacities to access it (or between different peoples' *tem-poralities* of access to "civilization"). The lowest degree of this differentiation reveals the existence of nonhuman-humans, those incapable of "entering history" and thus denied the capacity of taking the place of another. An analogous demonstration could undoubtedly be made concerning the effects of gender and moral and intellectual pathology. Universal humanity is not a *total* humanity; on the contrary, in an intensely paradoxical way "explained" by a philosophy of progress and a "pragmatic" anthropology of the inequality of abilities, universal humanity occupies only a *part* of the universe that it constructs.[16] Unlike the *synecdoche* that allows certain humans to be represented as *typical of humanity* as such, *totality* here is the equivalent of a *part*, albeit a massively dominant one.[17]

It is true that in the same period (several years later) a *different cosmopolitanism* emerges alongside Kant's, in which the relationship of unity to differences is to a certain extent reversed. This alternative cosmopolitism is that of the two von Humboldt brothers (the linguist Wilhelm and the geographer Alexander), whose work must be taken *together* in order to delineate the *universalism of differences* that the two of them describe (not for the first time, perhaps—Vico and Herder come to mind—but in a way that proves decisive for contemporary thought). This universalism could also be called, to borrow from Ernst Bloch, who adopted the term from Novalis, a *multiversum*.[18] As we shall see, although this alternative is very important, it ultimately underscores the aporetic nature of thinking the universal in its confrontation with differences. The overarching idea that unites the Humboldt brothers (and that undeniably runs counter to the Eurocentrism inherent in colonialization, even if European colonialization gave them the means to explore the multiplicity of human languages and the diversity of the "sites" or "environments" in which each culture discovers its specific equilibrium with nature) is the *equality of cultures* wherein cultures are considered creations of human genius, every one of which is indispensable to the history of humanity and to the great inventory of the planet's resources.[19] Yet the recognition of this equality in diversity (as it pertains to *cultural* difference) carries with it the conception of each culture or civilization as a closed, self-referential totality, whose uniqueness is expressed in its language and customs and, therefore, inevitably betrays an exclusive and normative character. Equality in diversity sanctions the belief that "all people are the same," but on the condition that each person remain attached to a *historical group* (or, to put it another way, a unique community of values and ways of thinking) outside of which they exist solely as alienated individuals, as strangers to themselves and to their own humanity. And, in accordance with a model that originates in Leibnizian "monadology" (and goes on to influence Benjamin and Lévi-Strauss), it also sanctions the belief that each culture provides a *unique point of view of the natural and human world* (and in this sense "partakes" of the universal), but at the price of an essential *impossibility of communication* (and a fortiori of mutual improvement) *between cultures*, which become something like autonomous "universes." It seems to me that, by way of comparison, we reach the heart of the aporia that is still with us today. Above I described the *uncertainty* (or anxiety, uneasiness) of subjects confronted with the multiplicity of human possibilities whose distribution they must negotiate within themselves and in their relations with others. The first aporia reveals that *there is no place* defined a priori in the economy of the world: neither in an economy that inscribes equality in a region of interchangeability by suppressing the threat of differences in the empirical or "concrete" world, nor in an economy that recognizes equality in difference (or, at least, in certain differences) while making separation (and protection or immunity) the condition on which the respect for this equality depends.

A similar aporia arises in the association of the notions of *community* and *universality*. While it is safe to say that all political philosophers of the modern and postrevolutionary age have dealt with this aporia, Hegel gives it its most radical expression. Because the wordplay of Hegel's terminology—*allgemein, Allgemeinheit,* and *Gemeinwesen*—tends to remain hidden when translated, my recourse to the original language is indispensable. Whereas French translations have made the German *allgemein* align with the logical and ethical notion of the *universal*, Hegel uses the term as the equivalent of Rousseau's "general will" (which is the will of the *community of citizens* who hold the "constituent power" of the state); above all, the term's etymology refers to that which is "common to all" (*allen gemein*).[20] What seems important here is that, based on this wordplay (which has nothing gratuitous about it), one can show that the *political community* requires the incorporation of universality into its laws and statutes (particularly in the form of individuals' *equal rights*), without which it can never be a "community of citizens" in the modern sense of the term (founded on the illimitation of the principle of equal freedom or on the illegitimacy of discrimination against members of the social body with regard to their political capacity, the latter expressed through participation and representation). But one can also show that universality must be realized within a community, because it becomes effective only when it is part of *institutions* that are themselves demanded and legitimized by a political community (or, as they said during the Age of Reason, part of a "constitution of freedom" that guarantees the right to rights).[21] There is, therefore, a very clear *reciprocity* of perspectives but no *coincidence* between the two requirements, neither with respect to institutions, nor with respect to the *objectives* or *aims* of political activism (which could be called *active citizenship*, or *citizenship through action*, akin to the "acts of citizenship" of a contemporary theorist like Engin Isin).[22]

Hegel gives a perfect description of the problem in speculative terms in his *Phenomenology of Spirit* (because in the *Elements of the Philosophy of Right*, by making the rule of law the effective realization of political rationality, Hegel seems to present the problem as resolved). He considers the problem as an *endless* succession of displacements between *communitarian closure* (which permits mutual recognition, through institutions, of the rights and duties common to all participants, who in turn constitute sovereign power) and *universalist openness* (which requires reconciliation with, if not the enemy, the "completely other," whether this other is present *within* the community or civic space as an excluded or "ironic" figure or enters it *from the outside*, in the way a foreigner seeks hospitality). Of course, we have already seen this oscillation in another form. That is no doubt why the demand for universality in contemporary communities of citizens (especially communities of citizens located on the *edge* of the nation-state's historical trajectory at a time when the traditional, legally sanctified equation of citizenship and nationality is no longer secure) alternatively—and occasionally, albeit contradictorily, *at the same time*—takes the form of a demand for *enlarging the community* in order to incorporate those whom it previously shut out (in particular foreigners and, in certain circumstances, "non-national" residents) as well as for a *dissolution of the community*, at least symbolically, in the form of a "community without community" or a "noncommunitarian being-in-common" (in other words, a community without *collective identity* serving as a precondition and norm of membership), a community, therefore, necessarily *without a state* (or emerging beyond the state and, possibly, beyond or on the faraway "shores" of the political).[23]

Another way to formalize the problem with which we are dealing (or to offer an allegory of it) would be to turn our attention to the word "we" in European grammar, a word whose ambiguity Émile Benveniste brings to light in his analysis of personal pronouns.[24] Benveniste's demonstration (which simultaneously functions as a kind of latent deconstruction) focuses on the equivocal and very nearly contradictory nature of the procedure by which a speaker moves from a first-person singular pronoun (the subject of enunciation par excellence, according to Benveniste, through which the speaker "appropriates language" by entering into a dialogical relationship with other speakers whose place, as in Kant, the subject may eventually take) to a "first-person plural" pronoun, which is supposed at once to name and present a *collective*. The *We* is a "first person" only if it implicitly includes an *I*, in other words, the *I* always *takes (a) place* in the *We*, which constitutes its real or imaginary "subjectivity." It goes without saying, however, that the *We* cannot be reduced to the *I*, for otherwise there would be nothing collective about it. Now, there are in language two antithetical interpretations of this collectivization. According to the first, the *We* designates the person who speaks as well as the person spoken to (the interlocutor), a situation that contains the rudiments of a community of interest, if not of properties ("you and I, we are speaking together," "we will leave together," "we will share the same roof and the same bread"). According to the second, the *We* designates the person who speaks *plus someone else*, a third party, distinct from and potentially antagonistic to the interlocutor ("he and I, we will see you later": either "we have to leave you now" or "we want nothing to do with you"), a situation that doesn't contain the rudiments of a community but rather, allegorically at least, the basis of a dissemination—that is, a move toward the universal whereby the universal is dissociated from a given community, or reconstitutes it elsewhere with no preexisting bonds. These observations go further than a denunciation of the transcendental illusion inherent in the "we" of institutional proclamations ("We the people," "We Europeans"), a denunciation that Jean-François Lyotard no less brilliantly provides in *The Differend*; that is, they go further than the critique of the imaginary representation of a common identity that seems to underlie every enunciation made *in the name* of a political collective.[25] Or, at least, they complete the critique. For while the inclusive, communitarian *We* entails the possibility of confinement in the Same, the exclusive universalizing *We* brings us back to the aporia of an indeterminate alterity that is at once completely other and completely alike, arousing a sense of both danger and solidarity. This brings to mind the turn of phrase with which Derrida (who claimed that it could "barely be translated and is perhaps perverse") once confronted Levinas: "every other is wholly other" ["tout autre est tout autre"].[26]

At this point, I would like to outline a third, more immediately political aporia, which, although a continuation of the second, I am calling the aporia of "co-citizenship." Rather than present it in a purely theoretical form, I would like to give it (at least partially) the form of a first-person narrative so as to stay as close as possible to the enunciative modalities in which the aporia has seemed to me unavoidable. In 1997, on the first anniversary of the occupation of Paris's Saint-Bernard Church by (mostly Malian and Senegalese) immigrants demanding both the legalization of their French residency status and work permits (that is, permits that would allow them to do what they had already been doing for years), I published a short text entitled "Ce que nous devons aux 'sans-papiers'" ["What We Owe the 'Undocumented'"], later republished in my essay collection *Droit de cité*.[27] In this text, I listed three "services" or "benefits" for which, I argued, "we" (French citizens) were indebted to the *sans-papiers*, who, from their hunger strikes to occupations of churches and other public buildings, had been tirelessly demanding the right to live and work in France. We were indebted to them, first, for having brought to public view, at the risk of reprisal, the reality of the conditions in which they lived and were exploited; second, for having refuted the racist myths that had spread about the reasons for their presence in France, thereby inaugurating a politics of truth with regard to the impact and usefulness of immigration; and, finally, for having created real political struggles and conflicts within the national space, their actions turning them into the *agents* of contemporary politics. I went on to describe them not as "citizens" in the legal sense of the term but as "co-citizens," who had ushered in new political solidarity beyond the institutional limits and definitions of passive citizenship imposed by state power. Ten years later (and in fact without my knowledge), the Austrian linguist and philosopher Stefan Nowotny, himself active in solidarity movements involving "illegal" immigrants in his own country, published a long essay in which he discussed my text in light of Benveniste's famous historical-philological argument regarding the "linguistic models of the city." He also raised an objection, which although amicable in form was quite formidable in content.[28]

By confronting my text with Benveniste's analysis, Nowotny undoubtedly attributed a much more radical, and in a way "epochal," meaning to my use of the term co-citizenship. Instead of appearing as a possible concession to public opinion (although you immigrants aren't exactly citizens, since you aren't a part of the national community legally defined, you *play the same role* politically as striking workers or union members and are, therefore, "in a way," co-citizens), the designation (which he rightly called an *interpellation* directed both at the *sans-papiers* themselves and, beyond them, at the entire political community) appeared in Nowotny's article as a subversive extension of the idea of citizenship, one whose foundation no longer depended on civil status or rights (inherited or acquired through naturalization) but on *securing political legitimacy* through struggle, action, and speech, provided that that struggle *coincided with* struggles that, in general, make citizens the inventors of the democracy to which they lay claim. To achieve this reversal of perspective, which, in a different terminology, one might call a move from constituted to constituent power, an intrinsic dimension of which seems to be a liberation from the *restrictions* that the nation-state imposes, Nowotny didn't turn to Benveniste for support but rather for inspiration. In doing so, he demonstrated the unexpectedly revolutionary significance that Benveniste's analysis might today assume.

Benveniste's argument is already familiar. According to the etymology, not only is the idea of the "Greek city" (*polis*) not identical to that of the Roman *civitas*, but the first is precisely the opposite of the second.[29] Indeed, the noun *civitas* comes *after* the noun *civis* (which we routinely translate as "citizen"); it expresses in an abstract way (like all terms ending in -*tas*: *voluptas, pietas, universitas*, etc.) a quality or property belonging to the *cives* without, however, preexisting them. On the other hand, in the Greek model (in the Greek language), things are reversed: The *politēs* (a word that, it should be noted, has practically no feminine) is a member of a preexisting *polis*, preceding the *politēs* just as a "whole" precedes its "parts" or "elements." Whereas the Greek terminology "says" that the city makes citizens, the Latin terminology says that the citizens make the city. Yet this is only the most extrinsic part of the demonstration, which could lead one to believe that the point is to highlight Roman individualism to the detriment of Greek organicism or holism, an idea fairly widespread in philosophy. Instead, Benveniste wants to show us something else when he *the linguist* (and I might even say the structuralist linguist, who reasons by way of semantic *oppositions*) asks the following question: What, in Latin, is the meaning of the word *civis*, from which the notion of *civitas* derives? The answer is that *civis* cannot mean "citizen" in the legal sense that we give the term, taking our cue from the letter of the Latin etymology but from the spirit of the "Greek" political model. The commonplace Latin expression *civis meus* shows this quite clearly. "My citizen" makes no sense; conversely, "my co-citizen" (which in English would be "my fellow citizen" and in German "mein Mitbürger") makes a great deal of sense (especially, I would add, when compared to the symmetrical expression *hostis meus*, either "my enemy" or "my host," depending on the context). What Nowotny looked to add to my formula was thus the idea that the *relation* between "co-citizens" such as it is established in shared political practice is the source of a refoundation of the city or, better, of citizenship. This refoundation circumvents the constituted definition of citizenship in order to enlarge that definition on different grounds ("neutralizing" the presupposition of the nation) through the creation of a political space specific to it. Nowotny took this to be a general characteristic of the *sans-papiers effect* in the crisis of European citizenship such as I had tried to express it in my description of the modalities of a "re-constitution of active citizenship" founded on the practices of resistance and activism themselves. At the same time, he suggested a dialectical way of resolving the aporia of the community such as I have outlined it above: by emphasizing the *universalization through action* of the community that occurs in every circumstance in which the community, in order to give life to politics within itself, is obliged to return to the "co-citizenship" of its origin or foundation by including, *by right*, the "other" (or the foreigner) who has been constitutionally excluded. This idea is of course totally compatible with the conception of politics as a collective practice of democracy that reemerges each time the "part of those who have no part" is affirmed.

At the same time, however, Nowotny presented a serious critique of my text. It was also based on Benveniste, in the role of theorist of *enunciation* in this case, and supported by references to Bakhtin.[30] Nowotny quite simply pointed out that "collective political practice," which underlies the idea of co-citizenship brought into the contemporary context, cannot be virtual, constructed on the abstract notion of a community of interests ("internationalist," for example), or on that of a "convergence of struggles" (in the terminology so dear to trade-union bureaucracy). Collective political practice presupposes actual dialogue between co-citizens. While no doubt full of good intentions, my interpellation of the "*sans-papiers* of Saint Bernard" looked in this respect more like a unilateral enunciation, a kind of *interrupted reciprocity* that threatened, for this very reason, to lapse into paternalism. Indeed, on the one hand, I proffered it *after the fact*, as the belated "acknowledgement of a debt," when the struggle itself had already come to an end. On the other, I stated it in the *language* (and rhetoric) of French politics, identifying the "benefit" that French politics had gained from the actions carried out by the immigrants or foreigners within it. Thus, the interpellation may have *objectively* had the opposite effect of the subversion initially imagined in considering Benveniste's "Roman model": Instead of contributing to the constitution of a new political subject, the interpellation merely requested, *through the intermediary of a fictional dialogue* with foreigners, a gesture of hospitality, that is to say, a *concession of rights* (or of "co-citizenship," to return to its narrow sense) from nationals who, in virtue of their dominant position, already possess those rights. The aporia of the universalization of the community thus appears as insurmountable as ever.[31]

"LES LANGUES SE PARLENT"

I can't say that I hold the key to resolving any of these aporias, and especially not the third, which very concretely involves the association of discourse and practice in the political field. Yet this last aporia seems to me to comprise, even by default, a dialectical aspect (because dialogical, that is, dialectical *in the element of speech*) that ought to illuminate the question of the universalism of differences. Such is the case if we return to the fundamental fact that the universal is not really a concept or an idea but rather *the correlate of an enunciation* that produces or fails to produce, depending on the circumstances, *an effect of universality* (or, to be still more precise, an effect of universality that *affirms differences*—including as a challenge to the domination of universality or as a conflict within the universal—or that denies or forbids their expression). Now, no *real* enunciation can be analyzed or interpreted independent of the *language* in which it is effectuated or, for that matter, independent of the multiplicity of languages within which the enunciation circulates—or *doesn't* circulate, a possibility to which Nowotny has drawn my attention with the notion of *interrupted reciprocity*.[32] This leads me to the hypothesis—post-Humboldtian, perhaps—that the most adequate *approximate* model of a *multiversum* (or of a "world" that makes room for difference as such, without *stabilizing* difference within impossible "identities") is furnished by the *linguistic multiplicity of humanity*. But provided that we bear in mind two notable conditions: (1) that this multiplicity is not *given* and does not remain *unchanged* (as it does in a table of "world languages" drawn up by comparative linguists or ethnolinguists) but rather is *transformed* by the act of translation (with its ineluctable relations of power or domination), which affects, although in different ways, both "source" and "target" languages (thus, little by little, all languages)[33]; and (2) that, in reality, in the practice of translation, it isn't so much individuals or social groups that communicate with one another but languages themselves that "*se parlent*" in a more or less uneasy, and sometimes violent, way. To conclude, I would like to explain briefly what I mean by this.[34]

There is of course no denying that individual subjects *make use* of one or more languages (or parts of them) for purposes that require usage more or less in conformity with, more or less deviant from, socially dominant or even politically imposed or codified standards. Individual usage is described by Benveniste as a process of appropriating language in which the decisive moment is enunciation, in other words, the fact that, here and now, a subject is established within the corpus of sentences of a given language in order to use its resources by designating her or himself in the first person. One might therefore assume that the act of translation, which involves *more than one language*, constitutes an intensified appropriation, or a second-order appropriation, in which the subject becomes the "owner" of several codes, or several instruments, with which she or he "plays" more or less effectively in order to enlarge the field of her or his communication. But this gets things backward, for the act of translation (or the entry into the "translation zone," as Emily Apter puts it) is much rather a paradoxical combination of appropriation and dispossession or relinquishment (to which Jacques Derrida applied, if he didn't coin, the oxymoronic notion of *ex-appropriation*).[35] This has nothing to do with any personal inadequacies on the part of translators (even if those inadequacies are sometimes glaring—although fundamentally no translator is ever "equal" to her or his task, as the best of them know perfectly well), but with the *impossibilities* and *inequalities* that are structurally inscribed in the relationship between languages and that nevertheless provide both the reason for and the means of translation.

Here again we encounter a double bind, one that unexpectedly recalls what I proposed above regarding the modality of anthropological differences (at once indestructible and unassignable), and that, as a consequence, encourages us to assign to translation, or to the relationship of translation that exists between languages themselves, the highest degree of *conflictual universality*. Indeed, as Barbara Cassin has patiently shown, languages are fundamentally untranslatable insofar as no perfect equivalence exists between their significations (or, to put it another way, they always comprise crucial elements of untranslatability, which reveal themselves as resistant to translation, as limits or stumbling blocks).[36] Furthermore, it is this untranslatability that opens languages to an infinite task of "impossible" translation, which is also, dialectically, a process that verifies their "idiomaticity" and a process by which they mutually develop or transform one another. But we might also say that in the practice of translation subjects contradictorily experience both the constraints of meaning and syntax, which cannot be transgressed "at will" (and which apply to *both* translating languages and translated languages), and the liberties, which one can and must take, drawing inspiration from a particular idiom, in order to transfer that idiom into another and, when necessary (as Benjamin explained in "The Task of the Translator," 1921), to transform a given language "poetically" so that it might admit the significations of another. Still, whatever subjects' freedom may be (whatever room for "play" they have or create for themselves), they are in all this merely the instruments or interpreters of the historical relation between languages themselves. The relation between constraints and liberties, the condition of possibility for the infinite translation of the untranslatable, lies at the level of languages. This is why I maintain that in translation it isn't subjects who speak to one another or who "speak in languages/tongues," as the Gospel writers put it (Acts 2:6), but more fundamentally languages that "*se parlent.*" And the clearer it is that translation in all its forms isn't an epiphenomenon of the multiplicity of languages but instead a *condition* of their interdependence and of their specific evolution, the clearer it will be that this reversal of perspective with regard to the current view of things is unavoidable (a reversal that could obviously be termed "anti-Copernican," since, once again, it *dislodges* the subject from its central position without, however, making it unnecessary or evanescent).

The very expression that I am using in French—"*les langues se parlent*"— provides an illustration. As with the desire to know (of which, I believe, translation itself is directly a part, as a *practice of difference* within the element of language), I am using this expression with an eye to one of Heidegger's famous formulations, whose basic idea we have to retain while radically correcting its underlying transcendentalism or theologism: *Die Sprache spricht* ("language speaks").[37] This phrase includes both the notion that "it is not man who speaks but language" and the idea that "language serves only to speak and nothing more," although speaking may be done either poetically, authentically (what Heidegger calls "the peal of stillness/silence," *das Geläut der Stille*), or inauthentically—that is, for utilitarian or everyday purposes, with a view to expression, conversation, or technical communication.[38] And yet, by employing an idiomatic particularity of French, which, although largely untranslatable, can be explained in neighboring languages (and which, I hope, will not be interpreted as a form of linguistic nationalism), I have subjected Heidegger's expression to an anthropological displacement. To say in French that *"les langues se parlent"* produces an intentional ambiguity because of the expressive identity between the impersonal and reciprocal forms of the verb (se *parler*). It means, in other words, both that *languages are spoken* by speakers and interlocutors (for example, "old Slavonic is still spoken [*se parle encore*] in certain regions," or "English is spoken [*se parle*] in Paris as much as in London"—which is doubtful) and that *languages speak among themselves* or *to one another* [*se parlent entre elles*], address one another, through the intermediary of translation (and, it goes without saying, of those who use these languages "in translation," whether to command or to serve and, in the worst case, *to silence* other languages, for no translation is ever egalitarian even if it imposes a certain reciprocity). In English, *languages are spoken* or *languages speak to one another*—this "nontranslation" is useful because it encourages us to keep these two aspects together: both the reversal that makes languages the starting point and end point of the *activity* that individuals undertake as they put themselves, so to speak, in the service of languages, and the idea that this reversal is experienced essentially by way of the reciprocity (once again, a fundamentally imperfect reciprocity, entwined with the power relations inherited from the past and maintained through politics) that makes certain languages "enter" into the life and history of other languages. Perhaps more than an allegory of the universal, this may be a way of stating practically and, at the same time, of constructing politically a certain type of universality in opposition to others in which multiplicity doesn't have the same constituent role, and in which the relations of domination are consequently less likely to be called into question and challenged.

We might therefore add another interpretation (which translation itself, acting as a gloss, should help to make clear): In generalized translation, languages "se parlent" (*sprechen einander, speak one another*), by degrees, at least in the mode of an "as if" (*as if* "French" spoke German, or "Hebrew" spoke Arabic, etc.). Which amounts to imagining that, by doubling the paradox of localization specific to every enunciation of the universal—the very paradox which, in the first chapter of *Phenomenology of Spirit*, Hegel places in the mouth of "language" itself—the indefinitely open totality of idioms (with the entirety of *relations* between them) constructs (but also endlessly deconstructs, reconstructs) universality beyond any unity. Because it is limited to defining a "site" of enunciation as the relation between *several* sites, or as the mobile term of a transfer from one language within another or several others, such a universality *frustrates its own enunciative paradox* by multiplying it. Or, to put things another way, it reverses the meaning of the paradox, turning a contradiction and a negative property of speaking beings into a method for constructing the universal and for moving beyond the particular, a method that is immanent to the historical singularity of discourses and to the unpredictable trajectories of their deterritorialization.

NOTES

1. RACISM, SEXISM, UNIVERSALISM: A REPLY TO JOAN SCOTT AND JUDITH BUTLER

1. The following essay is based on a lecture delivered at the University of Tokyo (Kamaba), October 9, 2002.

2. "Racism as Universalism," in *Masses, Classes, Ideas: Studies on Politics and Philosophy before and after Marx*, trans. James Swenson (New York: Routledge, 1994).

3. "Ambiguous Universality," in *Politics and the Other Scene*, trans. Christine Jones, James Swenson, and Chris Turner (London: Verso, 2002).

4. Françoise Duroux, "Une classe de femmes est-elle possible?" unpublished text, 1987. (A collection of Duroux's major essays is currently in preparation under the direction of Mireille Azzoug at Presses de l'Université de Vincennes-Saint Denis); Jean-Claude Milner, *Les Noms indistincts* (Paris: Le Seuil, 1983).

5. Judith Butler, *Excitable Speech: A Politics of the Performative* (New York: Routledge, 1997), 71–102.

6. Joan Wallach Scott, *Only Paradoxes to Offer: French Feminists and the Rights of Man* (Cambridge, Mass.: Harvard University Press, 1996).

7. Joan Wallach Scott, "Préface à l'édition française," *La Citoyenne paradoxale. Les Féministes françaises et les droits de l'homme*, trans. Marie Bourdé and Colette Pratt (Paris: Albin Michel, 1998), 12.

8. Étienne Balibar, *Equaliberty: Political Essays*, trans. James Ingram (Durham, N.C.: Duke University Press, 2014).

9. Michèle Duchet, *Anthropologie et histoire au siècle des Lumières* (Paris: Maspero, 1971).

10. This obviously brings to mind the entirety of Colette Guillaumin's work, which explores this relation (see in particular *Sexe, race et pratique du pouvoir. L'idée de nature* [Paris: Côté-femmes, 1992]).

11. See George L. Mosse, *Nationalism and Sexuality: Respectability and Abnormal Sexuality in Europe* (New York: Howard Fertig, 1985).

12. Étienne Balibar, "Racism and Nationalism," trans. Christ Turner, in É. Balibar and Immanuel Wallerstein, *Race, Nation, Class: Ambiguous Identities* (London: Verso, 1991).

13. Étienne Balibar, "De la préférence nationale à l'invention de la politique," in *Droit de cité* (Paris: Presses Universitaires de France, 2002 [1998]).

14. See the entirety of Geneviève Fraisse's work, beginning with *Reason's Muse: Sexual Difference and the Birth of Democracy*, trans. Jane Marie Todd (Chicago: The University of Chicago Press, 1994).

15. I reexamined this question in *Secularism and Cosmopolitanism*, trans. G. M. Goshgarian (New York: Columbia, 2018).

16. In *L'Avenir du christianisme* (Paris: Desclée de Brouwer, 1999), Stanislas Breton explains that a certain strand of Buddhism (which he studied in Kyoto) points the way to overcoming "religion" within Christianity itself.

17. I am obviously aligning myself here as closely as possible with the arguments of Jacques Rancière (*Disagreement*, trans. Julie Rose [Minneapolis: University of Minnesota Press, 1999]) concerning the opposition between the "police" (which assigns social *parts* while always excluding "those who have no part") and "politics" (which challenges the very principle of distribution by laying claim to "the part of those who have no part"). I would argue, however, that "politics" should name the contradictory unity of these two aspects rather than only *one* of the two poles.

18. In *Margins of Philosophy*, trans. Alan Bass (Chicago: The University of Chicago Press, 1972).

19. I have discussed these questions in a long essay, "Bourgeois Universality and Anthropological Differences" (initially published in the journal *L'Homme*), which serves as the conclusion to my book *Citizen Subject: Foundations for Philosophical Anthropology*, trans. Steven Miller (New York: Fordham University Press, 2017).

20. On this complex question as it appears in Foucault, see especially Stéphane Legrand's *Les Normes chez Foucault* (Paris: Presses Universitaires de France, 2007).

21. Jean-Luc Nancy, *The Inoperative Community*, trans. Peter Connor, Lisa Garbus, Michael Holland, and Simona Sawhney (Minneapolis: University of Minnesota Press, 1991); *The Disavowed Community*, trans. Philip Armstrong (New York: Fordham University Press, 2016).

2. CONSTRUCTIONS AND DECONSTRUCTIONS OF THE UNIVERSAL (FIRST LECTURE)

1. The present chapter combines two lectures, with some modifications, that I wrote at the same time and delivered, one shortly after the other, under same title (the first in English, the second in French) in March and April 2005. I took these

opportunities to try to clarify the same idea and to explore its implications. This explains the repetitions, which I hope the reader will forgive, but which I also hope will help reveal what can be teased out of a single working hypothesis in two different contexts and in two different languages.

This first lecture was delivered on March 24, 2005, at the Maison Française of New York University upon the invitation of Ms. Francine Goldenhar.

2. The expression "constructions of the universal" has been used, independently of my work, by Monique David-Ménard in her indispensable book on the relationship between philosophy and psychoanalysis, *Les Constructions de l'universel: psychanalyse, philosophie* (Paris: Presses Universitaires de France, 2009).

3. See Jacques Derrida, *Psyche: Inventions of the Other,* ed. Peggy Kamuf and Elizabeth Rottenberg (Stanford: Stanford University Press, 2007).

4. It should be noted that this notion is not without immediate critical value in an age of the oft-proclaimed "globalization" of the economy, politics, and culture. See Gérard Lebrun's major work, *La Patience du concept: Essai sur le discours hégélien* (Paris: Gallimard, 1972).

5. See especially Derrida's "The University without Condition," in *Without Alibi,* trans. Peggy Kamuf (Stanford: Stanford University Press, 2002); *Parages,* trans. Tom Conley, James Hulbert, John P. Leavey, and Avital Ronell (Stanford: Stanford University Press, 2010); and *Specters of Marx,* trans. Peggy Kamuf (New York: Routledge, 2006).

6. See Jacques Derrida, *"Khōra,"* in *On the Name,* trans. David Wood, John P. Leavey Jr., and Ian McLeod (Stanford: Stanford University Press, 1995).

7. Georg Wilhelm Friedrich Hegel, *Phenomenology of Spirit* (1807), trans. A. V. Miller (Oxford: Oxford University Press, 1977), Chapters V and VI.

8. Hegel, *Phenomenology of Spirit,* Chapter VI, Section C.

9. I have discussed these analyses in connection with Benveniste and Jean-Claude Milner (who acknowledges Benveniste's proximity to Hegel) in my book *Citizen Subject: Foundations for Philosophical Anthropology,* trans. Steven Miller (New York: Fordham University Press, 2017), Chapter 4 ("From Sense Certainty to the Law of Genre: Hegel, Benveniste, Derrida").

10. Michael Walzer, "Two Kinds of Universalism," in "Nation and Universe," *The Tanner Lectures on Human Values XI 1989,* ed. Grethe Peterson (Salt Lake City: University of Utah Press, 1990); Michael Walzer and David Miller, *Thinking Politically: Essays in Political Theory* (New Haven: Yale University Press, 2009); Étienne Balibar, "The Proposition of Equaliberty," in *Equaliberty: Political Essays,* trans. James Ingram (Durham, N.C.: Duke University Press, 2014).

11. Alain Badiou, *Saint Paul: The Foundation of Universalism,* trans. Ray Brassier (Stanford: Stanford University Press, 2003). Badiou generalizes the theological notion of *pistis* to the level of universalism in general, which for him

always follows the same model. Saint Paul thus foreshadows Lenin by way of the French Jacobins.

12. Derrida has thematized *exappropriation* in numerous essays, in particular: *Spurs: Nietzsche's Styles/Éperons: Les Styles de Nietzsche*, trans. Barbara Harlow (Chicago: The University of Chicago Press, 1979); *Given Time: I. Counterfeit Money*, trans. Peggy Kamuf (Chicago: The University of Chicago Press, 1992); *Monolingualism of the Other: or, The Prosthesis of Origin* (Stanford: Stanford University Press, 1998); with Bernard Stiegler, *Ecographies of Television*, trans. Jennifer Bajorek (Cambridge: Polity Press, 2002). See my commentary, "The Reversal of Possessive Individualism," in *Equaliberty: Political Essays*.

13. Jean-François Lyotard, *The Differend: Phrases in Dispute*, trans. Georges Van Den Abbeele (Minneapolis: University of Minnesota Press, 1988).

14. On the vicissitudes of Marx's and Engels's use of the term "ideology," see my study "The Vacillation of Ideology in Marxism," in *Masses, Classes, Ideas: Studies on Politics and Philosophy before and after Marx*, trans. James Swenson (New York: Routledge, 1994).

15. See Jacques Derrida, *Dissemination*, trans. Barbara Johnson (Chicago: The University of Chicago Press, 1981), 35–36. The formula, which continues to be very much misunderstood, signifies above all: no *other text* outside the text, in other words, no metalanguage.

16. Karl Marx and Friedrich Engels, *The German Ideology* (I. Feuerbach): "each new class which puts itself in the place of one ruling before it, is compelled [. . .] to represent its interest as the common interest of all the members of society, that is, expressed in ideal form: it has to give its ideas the form of universality" (New York: International Publishers, 1970), 65–66.

17. Foucault offered an initial outline of the concept in his preface to *The Birth of the Clinic* (1963) (trans. Alan Sheridan [London: Routledge, 2003], xxi), calling it "the common structure that carves up and articulates what is seen and what is said," which he would later generalize in *The Order of Things* (1966) and *The Archeology of Knowledge* (1969). The alignment with Marx makes clear that the transformation of a problematic of "knowledge" into a problematic of "power-knowledge" is an inevitable dialectical development.

18. More precisely: "The ideas (*Gedanken*) of the ruling class are in every epoch the ruling ideas (*die herrschenden Gedanken*), i.e., the class which is the ruling *material* force of society, is at the same time its ruling *intellectual* force (*herrschende geistige Macht*)" (*The German Ideology*, 64). The Marxist tradition duly registered that ideology is here defined by Marx as a system of autonomous ideas and thus reformulated the thesis in terms of ideology.

19. Now republished with the full manuscript from which it was initially excerpted in 1970: *On the Reproduction of Capitalism*, trans. G. M. Goshgarian (London: Verso, 2014). The near simultaneity of Althusser's essay and Pierre

Bourdieu and Jean-Claude Passeron's *Reproduction in Education, Society and Culture* (trans. Richard Nice [London: Sage Publications, 2000]) is worth noting, even if it merits development elsewhere. Unlike Althusser, however, the latter authors seek to autonomize the moment of "symbolic violence."

20. Karl Marx, *Capital*, vol. I, trans. Ben Fowkes (New York: Penguin Books, 1990); see Parts 1 and 2, especially, 178–80 and 279–80.

21. I have already outlined this "reversal" of the standard interpretation of the Marxist thesis in a text devoted to Althusser, "Le non-contemporain" (1987), republished in *Écrits pour Althusser* (Paris: La Découverte, 1991). Pierre Macherey has recently revisited the central parts of the question in his book *Le Sujet des normes* (Paris: Éditions Amsterdam, 2014), incorporating them into his own interpretation of Marx's formula, which places it in proximity with Foucault and Bourdieu with regard to the "normalizing" function.

22. On this point, see Marx's two critiques of Hegel from 1843 (known as the Kreuznach manuscript, "Critique of Hegel's Doctrine of the State") and 1844 (his introduction to *Critique of Hegel's "Philosophy of Right"*).

23. Jean-François Lyotard laid the groundwork for an analysis of this "paralogism of the we," symmetrical to the paralogism that Kant examines in the *Critique of Pure Reason* with regard to the "I," in a remarkable passage of his book *The Differend* (No. 155).

24. Jean-Claude Milner, *Les Noms indistincts* (Paris: Éditions du Seuil, 1983), Chapter 11 ("Les classes paradoxales").

25. Joan Wallach Scott, *Only Paradoxes to Offer: French Feminists and the Rights of Man* (Cambridge, Mass.: Harvard University Press, 1997); Françoise Duroux, "Une classe de femmes est-elle possible?" (unpublished text), 1987 (also see her two books, on Antigone and Virginia Woolf: *Antigone encore. Les Femmes et la loi* [Paris: Côté-femmes, 1993] and *Virginia Woolf: Identité, politique, écriture* [Paris: Indigo et Côté-femmes, 2008]).

26. Baruch Spinoza, *Ethics*, Part V, Proposition XXXVI.

27. Ideally, the reader would refer to the original version of the essay first published in the review *La Pensée* 151 (June 1970) or to the essay collection *Positions (1964–1975)* (Paris: Éditions Sociales, 1976) in which the original is reprinted. Its republication in *On the Reproduction of Capitalism* (trans. G. M. Goshgarian [London: Verso, 2014]), carried out under Jacques Bidet's editorial care, has the advantage of providing variants (which are often quite interesting) and the context of the manuscript that Althusser took it from, but also the inconvenience of eliminating the traces of the essential textual breaks that are necessary for the text's intelligibility.

28. Note that Rousseau's idiomatic "general" is the point of intersection (or perhaps of indistinction) between two meanings into which, for "us" French speakers, the Hegelian term *All(en)gemeinheit* is divided: the common to all and

the universal. It thus exactly prefigures the term's internal dialectic. See the two chapters I devote to Hegel in *Citizen Subject*, Part II ("Being(s) in Common").

29. Essay republished in Balibar, *Masses, Classes, Ideas*.

2. CONSTRUCTIONS AND DECONSTRUCTIONS OF THE UNIVERSAL (SECOND LECTURE)

1. This essay is based on a lecture delivered at the plenary session of the 20th and 21st Century French and Francophone Studies International Colloquium, "Verbal, Visual, Virtual: New Canons for the Twenty-first Century," on April 1, 2005, at the France-Florida Institute, University of Florida, Gainesville.

2. Foucault describes *parrhēsia* in its dual "aspects" (philosophical and political) as a specific modality of *veridiction* and as the precursor to the modern notion of "critique." See his lectures at the Collège de France from 1983 to 1984: *The Courage of Truth: The Government of Self and Others II*, trans. Graham Burchell (London: Palgrave Macmillan, 2011) and at the University of Louvain from 1981, *Wrong-Doing, Truth-Telling*, trans. Stephen W. Sawyer (Chicago: The University of Chicago Press, 2014), as well as my commentary, "Speak Truth to Power," *The Journal of Contemporary Thought* 39 (Summer 2014).

3. Jean-Jacques Rousseau, *The Social Contract* (1761), trans. Christopher Betts (Oxford: Oxford University Press, 1999), Book 2, Chapter 6 ("The Law"), 73–74.

4. See especially her contribution to the discussion with Ernesto Laclau and Slavoj Žižek in *Contingency, Hegemony, Universality: Contemporary Dialogues on the Left* (London: Verso, 2000).

5. Blaise Pascal, *Pensées*, trans. W. F. Trotter (New York: Random House, 1941), § 294: "On what shall man found the order of the world which he would govern? Shall it be on the caprice of each individual? What confusion! Shall it be on justice? Man is ignorant of it. Certainly had he known it, he would not have established this maxim, the most general of all that obtain among men, that each should follow the customs of his own country. The glory of true equity would have brought all nations under subjection, and legislators would not have taken as their model the fancies and caprice of Persians and Germans instead of this unchanging justice. We would have seen it set up in all the States on earth and in all times; whereas we see neither justice nor injustice which does not change its nature with change in climate. Three degrees of latitude reverse all jurisprudence; a meridian decides the truth. Fundamental laws change after a few years of possession; right has its epochs; the entry of Saturn into the lion marks to us the origin of such and such a crime. A strange justice that is bounded by a river! Truth on this side of the Pyrenees, error on the other side."

6. Pascal, *Pensées*, § 858.

7. See my commentary in *Pascal et Spinoza. Pensées du contraste: de la géométrie du hasard à la nécessité de la liberté*, ed. Laurent Bove, Gérard Bras, and Éric Méchoulan (Paris: Éditions Amsterdam, 2007). Alain Badiou uses this provocative "pensée" as the epigraph to Meditation Twenty-One of his book *Being and Event* (trans. Oliver Feltham [London: Continuum, 2005], 212), where, as part of his interpretation of Pascal, an analysis of the *possibility* of the event turns into its *nomination* (and thus into its recognition and into the fidelity that the event requires).

8. I am purposefully using this term in reference to Alain Badiou's book on Saint Paul: *Saint Paul: The Foundation of Universalism*, trans. Ray Brassier (Stanford: Stanford University Press, 2003).

9. Étienne Balibar, *Equaliberty: Political Essays*, trans. James Ingram (Durham, N.C.: Duke University Press, 2014).

10. Michael Walzer, "Nation and Universe," *The Tanner Lectures on Human Values XI 1989*, ed. G. Peterson (Salt Lake City: University of Utah Press, 1990), published in French in *Esprit* 187 (December 1992). In his recent book, *L'Universel en éclats* (Lagrasse, France: Editions Verdier, 2014), Jean-Claude Milner identifies the "intense" or "singular" universal with the discourse that "affirms the Jewish name"; opposed to this intensive universal is the extensive or "plural" universal, the latter founded on the union of a multiplicity within a unique law or denomination (such as the *nomen Romanum*). According to Milner, this disjunction is the result of a "rupture" produced within Greek thought and civilization by Alexander the Great, uniting all the subjects (Greeks or Barbarians) of his empire in a single affiliation with the cosmos, and which Saint Paul would inherit in his famous "neither Jew nor Greek." Milner corroborated this dialectic of opposites— of the "Jewish name" and the *nomen Romanum* (or, if one prefers, Election and Empire)—during our discussion of his book at the Collège International de Philosophie on May 30, 2015.

11. In a brilliant essay on the philosophical and political presuppositions underlying Benveniste's theorization of "subjectivity in language," Jean-Claude Milner shows that Benveniste drew inspiration from Hegel's chapter on "sense certainty." See "*Ibat obscurus*" in *Le Périple structural: Figures et paradigme* (Paris: Seuil, 2002).

12. Georg Wilhelm Friedrich Hegel, *Phenomenology of Spirit* (1807), trans. A. V. Miller (Oxford: Oxford University Press, 1977), Chapter VI. *Entfremdet* is translated in French by Jean Hyppolite with the more classical "alienated" and by Jean-Pierre Lefebvre as "estranged" ["*étrangé*"] (in the sense of having become a stranger to oneself), which is closer to a Derridean reading.

13. "The movement of the ethical powers against each other and of the individualities calling them into life and action have attained their true end only in so far as both sides suffer the same destruction. For neither power has any advantage

over the other that would make it a more essential moment of the substance. [. . .] Only in the downfall of both sides alike is absolute right accomplished, and the ethical substance as the negative power which engulfs both sides, that is, omnipotent and righteous Destiny, steps on the scene." Hegel, *Phenomenology of Spirit*, 285.

14. "*Die Aufklärung*," an expression that Hegel himself puts in quotation marks and that, through his elucidation of the term, he contributes to making a category of historical interpretation that is itself universal. See Jean Hyppolite's indispensable commentary, *Genesis and Structure of Hegel's "Phenomenology of Spirit,"* trans. Samuel Cherniak and John Heckman (Evanston, Ill.: Northwestern University Press, 1979).

15. "As a result, faith has lost the content which filled its element, and collapses into a state in which it moves listlessly to and fro within itself. [. . .] Faith has, in fact, become the same as Enlightenment, viz. the consciousness of the relation of what is in itself finite to an Absolute without predicates, an Absolute unknown and unknowable; but there is this difference, the latter is *satisfied* Enlightenment, but faith is *unsatisfied* Enlightenment." Hegel, *Phenomenology of Spirit*, 349.

16. Susan Buck-Morss, *Hegel, Haiti, and Universal History* (Pittsburgh: University of Pittsburgh Press, 2009).

17. "It is this fact that guides the entire series of patterns of consciousness in their necessary sequence. But it is just this necessity itself, or the *origination* of the new object, that presents itself to consciousness without its understanding how this happens, which proceeds for us, as it were, behind the back of consciousness." Hegel, *Phenomenology of Spirit*, 56.

18. The idea that we can always read directly in Hegel's text a *remainder* not incorporated into Absolute Knowledge, and in particular a remainder of temporality heterogeneous to the dialectic of the "sublation" (*Aufhebung*) of oppositions and contradictions, is the guiding theme of Derrida's commentary, or rather the "column," he devotes to Hegel in *Glas* (1974).

19. Hegel, *Phenomenology of Spirit*, Chapter VI, Section A ("The *True* Spirit. The Ethical Order"), 266–94.

20. Hegel, *Phenomenology of Spirit*, Chapter VI, Section B ("Self-alienated Spirit. Culture"), 294–363.

21. Hegel, *Phenomenology of Spirit*, Chapter VI, Section B:III ("Absolute Freedom and Terror"), 355–63.

22. See Bertrand Ogilvie's study "Violence et représentation: La Production de l'homme-jetable" (1995) (republished in *L'homme jetable. Essai sur l'exterminisme et la violence extrême* [Paris: Amsterdam, 2012]) and Rebecca Comay's *Mourning Sickness: Hegel and the French Revolution* (Stanford: Stanford University Press, 2011).

23. See her recent book *Parting Ways: Jewishness and the Critique of Zionism* (New York: Columbia University Press, 2012).

24. See Gayatri Spivak, *A Critique of Postcolonial Reason: Towards a History of the Vanishing Present* (Cambridge, Mass.: Harvard University Press, 1999). A partial French translation, based on an earlier essay, was published by Éditions Amsterdam in 2009 (*Les Subalternes peuvent-elles parler?*).

25. See Étienne Balibar, "The Vacillation of Ideology in Marxism," in *Masses, Classes, Ideas: Studies on Politics and Philosophy before and after Marx*, trans. James Swenson (New York: Routledge, 1994).

26. See my study, "The Invention of the Superego: Freud and Kelsen, 1922," in *Citizen Subject: Foundations for Philosophical Anthropology*, trans. Steven Miller (New York: Fordham University Press, 2017).

27. Thomas Mann, *Betrachtungen eines Unpolitischen* [Reflections of a Nonpolitical Man], 1918.

28. On this point, see Georges Canguilhem's essay, "La Décadence de l'idée de progrès," in *Revue de Métaphysique et de morale* 92, no. 4 (1987).

3. *SUB SPECIE UNIVERSITATIS*: SPEAKING THE UNIVERSAL IN PHILOSOPHY

1. The present text is an adaption of the article "*Sub specie universitatis*," published initially (in English) in a special issue of the review *Topoi* (25 [2006]) dedicated to the theme "Philosophy: What Is to Be Done?" edited by Ermanno Bencivenga. A partial French translation, by Pierre Rusch, which I have largely borrowed from here, was published online in the review *Transeuropéennes* (fall 2009) (http://transeuropeennes.org/fr/articles/101).

2. Among the numerous philosophical essays recently published on the question of the university, I would like to point out two that seem to me equally valuable although they offer very different analyses: Jacques Derrida, "The University without Condition," in *Without Alibi*, trans. Peggy Kamuf (Stanford: Stanford University Press, 2002) and Pierre Macherey, *La Parole universitaire* (Paris: La Fabrique, 2011).

3. Gilles Deleuze and Félix Guattari, *What Is Philosophy?* trans. Hugh Tomlinson and Graham Burchell (New York: Columbia University Press, 1994), Chapter 4; Giorgio Agamben, Alain Badiou, Étienne Balibar, et al., *Penser l'Europe à ses frontières. Géophilosophie de l'Europe* (La-Tour-D'aigues: Éditions de l'Aube, 1998).

4. François Jullien, *De l'universel, de l'uniforme, du commun et du dialogue entre les cultures* (Paris: Fayard, 2008).

5. Asking whether there are "philosophies" outside Western culture (which in this case includes the whole Arabic-Persian tradition) is no less circular than asking whether forms of "monotheism" exist outside the Jewish-Christian-Islamic genealogy (moreover, the two questions may not be unrelated): The category that

dictates the research method is precisely the one upon which the research is focused. See Kenta Ohji and Mikhaïl Xifaras, *Éprouver l'universel: Essai de géophilosophie* (Paris: Klimé, 1999).

6. Only one other discipline would later come close to this supreme status: "dialectical materialism," as it was defined and sanctified in socialist countries from the 1930s to the 1980s. This science remained rather unproductive, and never rose to the level of its medieval model, although it aroused a certain nostalgia in the Catholic Church, which Stanislas Breton humorously recounts in his intellectual autobiography, *De Rome à Paris. Itinéraire philosophique* (Paris: Desclée de Brouwer, 1992).

7. Comparisons between Spinoza and Wittgenstein were part of the philosophical zeitgeist for a time. They have now found a top-notch artisan: Aristides Baltas, *Peeling Potatoes or Grinding Lenses: Spinoza and Young Wittgenstein Converse on Immanence and Its Logic* (Pittsburgh: University of Pittsburgh Press, 2012).

8. See the article "Praxis" in the *Dictionary of Untranslatables: A Philosophical Lexicon*, eds. Barbara Cassin, Emily Apter, Jacques Lezra, and Michael Wood (Princeton: Princeton University Press, 2014) (the section of the article devoted to Wittgenstein was written by Sandra Laugier).

9. In Propositions 6.431 to 6.45 of the *Tractatus*, Wittgenstein (correctly) interprets the Spinozist viewpoint *sub specie aeterni* as an eternity of presence in the world in the present moment (excluding one's imaginings of death) and reserves the qualification "mystical" for the pure position of the world as "fact."

10. It is acknowledged today that the idea of "double truth" does not appear in these terms in Averroes (Ibn Rushd), even though an entire tradition coming out of Thomism believed to have found it in the *Decisive Treatise*. And yet this is precisely where we need to look for the origin of the strategy of disjunction of universals. See Ali Benmakhlouf, *Averroès* (Paris: Les Belles Lettres, 2000); Luca Bianchi, *Pour une histoire de la "double vérité"* (Paris: Vrin, 2008).

11. From the first chapter of the *Phenomenology* ("Sense Certainty"), Hegel endows "consciousness" with a linguistic capacity that is the condition for its self-reflexive description—an equivalence that Marx, in *The German Ideology*, will attempt to deduce from materialist premises.

12. *"Ich, das Wir, und Wir, das Ich ist"*: *Phenomenology of Spirit*, trans. A. V. Miller (Oxford: Oxford University Press, 1997), Chapter IV. See my commentary in *Citizen Subject: Foundations for Philosophical Anthropology*, trans. Steven Miller (New York: Fordham University Press, 2017), Chapter 5 (*"Ich, das Wir, und Wir, das Ich ist*: Spirit's Dictum").

13. See Karl Marx, *Capital*, vol. 3, Chapter 27, "The Role of Credit in Capitalist Production."

14. Which brings to mind Freud's dialectical formulation in *New Introductory Lectures on Psycho-Analysis* from 1932: "Where id was, there ego shall be."

15. On the successive conceptions of translation in Western history and the "problems of translation" that they themselves raise, see especially the long entry "To Translate" in the *Dictionary of Untranslatables*. Also see Emanuela Fornari's reflections on the reciprocity of the notions of "translation" and "transition," in *Line di confine. Filosofia e postcolonialismo* (Turin: Bollati Boringhieri, 2008).

16. Notably, this is Paul Ricoeur's starting point to one of his last essays (on a theme that interested him throughout his life): *On Translation*, trans. Eileen Brennan (New York: Routledge, 2006).

17. Reprinted as Chapter 2, "Translation and Meaning," of his book *Word and Object* (1960) (Cambridge, Mass.: MIT Press, 2013).

18. Among many insightful commentaries on Quine and the discussions his essay provoked, I owe a particular debt of gratitude to Sandra Laugier's book, *L'Anthropologie logique de Quine. L'Apprentissage de l'obvie* (Paris: Vrin, 1992).

19. See the English translation in *Selected Writings, 1: 1913–1926*, ed. Marcus Bullock and Michael W. Jennings (Cambridge, Mass.: Belknap Press, 2004).

20. Benjamin's essay was initially published in 1923, as the preface to his translation of Baudelaire's *Tableaux parisiens*. See the magnificent "reconstruction" of Benjamin's unfinished (or imaginary) *Baudelaire*, edited by Giorgio Agamben, Barbara Chitussi, and Clemens-Carl Härle, with an introduction by Agamben (Paris: La Fabrique, 2013).

21. The idea of the community of languages as an infinite effect of translation practices, in which their affinity constitutes an event eternally "to come" rather than a legacy of the past, bears striking analogies to the Derridean concept of "exappropriation." It is all the more surprising, then, to see Derrida, in his essay "Des tours de Babel" (1985), so vehemently criticize the thesis of "pure language"; he apparently misunderstands Benjamin's final considerations concerning the translation of the Scriptures as literal transcription (*verbum pro verbo*), and seems to believe that they are meant to illustrate the same thesis. In my view, they introduce an ironic antithesis. "Des tours de Babel," trans. Joseph F. Graham, republished in *Psyche: Inventions of the Other*, vol. 1 (Stanford: Stanford University Press, 2007).

22. Much of what follows liberally draws on notions initially developed in pragmatic linguistics and sociolinguistics that are now part of a broad consensus. Jean-Jacques Lecercle, a French linguist and philosopher, author of *Interpretation as Pragmatics* (New York: St. Martin's Press, 1999), offers an illuminating synthesis of these debates in *A Marxist Philosophy of Language*, trans. Gregory Elliott (Leiden: Brill, 2006).

23. Mikhail Bakhtin, *The Dialogic Imagination*, ed. Michael Holquist, trans. Caryl Emerson and Michael Holquist (Austin: University of Texas Press, 1981).

24. Étienne Balibar, "Europe as Borderland," The Alexander von Humboldt Lecture in Human Geography, University of Nijmegen, November 10, 2004 (http://gpm.ruhosting.nl/avh/Europe%20as%20Borderland.pdf). Republished in *Society and Space* 27, no. 2 (2009).

25. Among whose names, from a philosophical perspective, Judith Butler also belongs. See, for example, "Restaging the Universal: Hegemony and the Limits of Formalism," in Judith Butler, Ernesto Laclau, and Slavoj Žižek, *Contingency, Hegemony, Universality: Contemporary Dialogues on the Left* (London: Verso, 2000).

26. Let us note the recent translation into French of several of Gayatri Spivak's books, notably *En d'autres mondes, en d'autres mots* (2009) (*In Other Worlds: Essays in Cultural Politics*, 1987), although we are still waiting for the complete translation of *A Critique of Postcolonial Reason*. Homi Bhabha's *The Location of Culture* (1994) was finally published in French in 2007. But there seems to be no progress on a translation of Naoki Sakai's *Translation and Subjectivity: On Japan and Cultural Nationalism* (Minneapolis: University of Minnesota Press, 1997) or of his more recent work, although some is available in French online.

27. Claude Lévi-Strauss's extraordinary achievement in *Mythologiques* is to have shown that the totality of American-Indian myths (at least those that have been recorded) can be situated within a relationship of "mutual translation," because each of them, as narrative, directly or indirectly derives from any of the others via the application of certain semantic rules. This idea (which is not unrelated to Benjamin's "pure language") could perhaps be extended to other "phrase regimens." It neglects, however, the conflictual dimension of the transformations. See Patrice Maniglier, "L'Humanisme interminable de Claude Lévi-Strauss," *Le Temps modernes* 609 (June–August 2000): 216–41.

28. Zygmunt Bauman, *In Search of Politics* (Cambridge: Polity Press, 1999), 202.

29. Jean-François Lyotard, *The Differend: Phrases in Dispute*, trans. Georges Van Den Abbeele (Minneapolis: University of Minnesota Press, 1988).

30. See Remo Bodei, *Multiversum. Tempo e storia in Ernst Bloch* (Nales: Bibliopolis, 1979). Bloch's essay, in which the notion of the *multiversum* first appears (a long-distance borrowing from Novalis, who made it the middle term of a syllogism between *universum* and *omniversum*), was presented in 1955 before the GDR Academy of Science (where, we might imagine, it was coolly received) with the title *"Differenzierungen im Begriff Fortschritt"* (see Ernst Bloch, *Tübinger Einleitung in die Philosophie*, vol. 1 [Frankfurt am Main: Suhrkamp, 1964], 160–202). 2016—After revising this essay, I became aware of John Leavitt's book *Linguistic Relativities: Language Diversity and Modern Thought* (Cambridge: Cambridge University Press, 2011), in which one chapter is entitled "Boas and the Linguistic Multiverse." Although the author gives no reference for the term, he uses it in a way completely compatible with what I have proposed here.

4. ON UNIVERSALISM: IN DIALOGUE WITH ALAIN BADIOU

1. The following is my keynote address to a discussion organized by the School of Social Sciences, University of California, Irvine, February 2, 2007 ("2007 Koehn Event in Critical Theory. A Dialogue between Alain Badiou and Étienne Balibar on 'Universalism'").

2. Some time prior to our discussion, Badiou had "axiomatized" his conception of the universal; see "Eight Theses on the Universal" (2000), *Theoretical Writings*, trans. and ed. Ray Brassier and Alberto Toscano (London: Continuum, 2004). However, my references, explicit or implicit, are above all to *Being and Event* (1988) and *Saint Paul: The Foundation of Universalism* (1997). I have already discussed different aspects of Badiou's project in "The History of Truth: Alain Badiou in French Philosophy," trans. David Macey, in *Think Again: Alain Badiou and the Future of Philosophy*, ed. Peter Hallward (London: Continuum, 2004).

3. See my previous essays: "Racism as Universalism," in *Masses, Classes, Ideas: Studies on Politics and Philosophy before and after Marx*, trans. James Swenson (New York: Routledge, 1994); "Ambiguous Identities," in *Politics and the Other Scene*, trans. Christine Jones, James Swenson, and Chris Turner (London: Verso, 2002); "*Sub Specie Universitatis*: Speaking the Universal in Philosophy," first published in English in *Topoi* 25 (2006) and adapted as Chapter 3 above.

4. "Racism and Nationalism," trans. Chris Turner, in Étienne Balibar and Immanuel Wallerstein, *Race, Nation, Class: Ambiguous Identities* (London: Verso, 1991).

5. I am especially thinking of the successive "dialectics" of divine law and human law (Antigone and Creon) and of the "dialectic" of faith and insight as forms of culture (the Enlightenment) in the *Phenomenology of Spirit*.

6. Étienne Balibar, "The Proposition of Equaliberty," in *Equaliberty: Political Essays*, trans. James Ingram (Durham: Duke University Press, 2014).

7. Michael Walzer, "Nation and Universe," *The Tanner Lectures on Human Values XI 1989*, ed. Grethe Peterson (Salt Lake City: University of Utah Press, 1990), delivered at Brasenose College, Oxford University, May 1 and 8, 1989.

8. Alain Badiou, *Saint Paul: The Foundation of Universalism*, trans. Ray Brassier (Stanford: Stanford University Press, 2003). Badiou also presents the notion of the *simulacrum* in *Ethics: An Essay on the Understanding of Evil*, trans. Peter Hallward (London: Verso, 2001).

9. See the chapter "Meditation Thirty-Two: Rousseau," in Alain Badiou, *Being and Event*, trans. Oliver Feltham (London: Continuum, 2005).

10. Dipesh Chakrabarty, *Provincializing Europe: Postcolonial Thought and Historical Difference* (Princeton: Princeton University Press, 2000).

11. See Giovanna Borradori, *Philosophy in a Time of Terror: Dialogues with Jürgen Habermas and Jacques Derrida* (Chicago: The University of Chicago Press, 2003).

12. It is interesting to note, as a recent study by Ishay Rosen-Zvi and Adi Ophir indeed seems to demonstrate ("Paul and the Invention of the Gentiles," *The Jewish Quarterly Review* 105, no. 1 [Winter 2015]: 1–41), that Saint Paul invented the generic distinction between Jews and *Goyim*, a distinction later mirrored and sanctioned by the rabbinic tradition. Thus, in order to "deny" a difference from a certain point of view (which will thereby articulate the universal), Saint Paul is obliged to begin by *constituting* that difference as such, and therefore to perpetuate it in the form of a negation.

13. See Frieder O. Wolf's essay "The International Significance of the Levellers," in Tony Benn and Frieder O. Wolf, *The International Significance of the Levellers and the English Democratic Tradition* (Nottingham: Spokesman Books, 2000).

14. See Balibar, "The Proposition of Equaliberty."

15. Hannah Arendt, "The Decline of the Nation-State and the End of the Rights of Man," in *The Origins of Totalitarianism* (New York: Harcourt Brace, 1973), Part Two ("Imperialism"), Chapter 9. Astoundingly (but not innocently), Part Two was long omitted from the French translation of Arendt's masterwork. From the 1950s to 1970s, the genealogy of antisemitism and the comparative study of Nazi and Communist "totalitarianisms" may have been admissible in France, but not the idea that the colonial system formed the intermediary link in this chain of extermination.

16. Jacques Rancière, *Disagreement*, trans. Julie Rose (Minneapolis: University of Minnesota Press, 1999); Maurice Merleau-Ponty, "A Note on Machiavelli," in *Signs*, trans. Richard C. McClearly (Evanston: Northwestern University Press, 1964). The expression "power of the powerless" was also taken up by Václav Havel in texts written for Charter 77 after the suppression of the Prague Spring.

17. In a terminology I have used elsewhere, I would argue that the corresponding political problem not only has to do with emancipation or transformation but with *civility*: Étienne Balibar, *Violence and Civility: On the Limits of Political Philosophy*, trans. G. M. Goshgarian (New York: Columbia University Press, 2015).

18. See Max Weber, *The Vocation Lectures*, trans. Rodney Livingstone (Indianapolis: Hackett Publishing, 2014).

5. A NEW QUARREL

1. A version of this essay, adapted to serve as the conclusion to the present book, was first presented as the closing address at the conference "Thinking Universalities," organized by the journal *Philosophy Today* and DePaul University in Chicago (with the additional support of the Department of Philosophy of Kingston University, London), October 23–24, 2015.

2. The expression, to which I return below, is "untranslatable" in philosophical languages otherwise close to French, notably German and English. This is why it is important, as we elucidate the expression, to work with its partial and defective "translations," which reproduce within translation the strategy of translation itself.

3. Étienne Balibar, *Citizen Subject*, trans. Steven Miller (New York: Fordham University Press, 2017), Chapter 14 ("Bourgeois Universality and Anthropological Differences").

4. See my chapter "The Proposition of Equaliberty" in *Equaliberty: Political Essays*, trans. James Ingram (Durham, NC: Duke University Press, 2014).

5. I am obviously distinguishing in principle between the idea of "neutralizing" anthropological differences in certain "jurisdictions" (for example, in the exercise of political citizenship) and the fact of "abolishing" them in practice or in thought. The distinction here goes to the heart of modern universalism, which I call "civil-bourgeois." Yet all the aporias internal to this universalism are connected, in one way or another, to the uncertain limits between these two attitudes.

6. Jacques Derrida very much insisted on the metaphysical character of this foundation both in his posthumous work *The Animal That Therefore I Am* (published thanks to Marie-Louise Mallet's dedicated work) (trans. David Wills [New York: Fordham University Press, 2008]) and in his lectures: *The Beast and the Sovereign*, vol. 1 (2001–2002), trans. Geoffrey Bennington (Chicago: The University of Chicago Press, 2009) and *The Beast and the Sovereign*, vol. 2 (2002–2003), trans. Geoffrey Bennington (Chicago: The University of Chicago Press, 2011).

7. Francis Wolff, *Notre Humanité. D'Aristote aux neurosciences* (Paris: Fayard, 2010).

8. See, for example, Donna Haraway's speculations about the "cyborg," which began with her essay "A Cyborg Manifesto: Science, Technology, and Socialist-Feminism in the Late Twentieth Century" (1984), republished in *Simians, Cyborgs, and Women: The Reinvention of Nature* (New York: Routledge 1991). Also see Thierry Hoquet, *Cyborg philosophie: Penser contre les dualismes* (Paris: Le Seuil, 2011).

9. One of the most important aspects of the breakdown of the "national model" of human diversity, to which I return below, is that one no longer takes for granted even a potential correspondence between "ethnic community" and "linguistic community," or, to put it another way, *language has been deterritorialized*, a topic that Deleuze and Guattari examine in a very beautiful chapter of *A Thousand Plateaus*, "Postulates of Linguistics," trans. Brian Massumi (Minneapolis: University of Minnesota Press, 1987).

10. Faulkner is the foremost novelist of this intersection, and particularly so in his masterpiece *Absalom, Absalom!* (1936). Rather than "interférence," the

term I used in the initial French version of this essay, many contemporary French theorists of feminism and postcolonialism, adapting Anglophone terminology, prefer to speak of "intersection" or "intersectionnalité." See Hourya Bentouhami-Molino, *Race, Cultures, Identités. Une approche féministe et postcoloniale* (Paris: PUF, 2015).

11. Unless we take the category of ideology in the sense suggested by Althusser (which is far from the original Marxist sense) as individuals' representation of the imaginary (or "lived") relationship to their conditions of social existence (and we must recognize, of course, that this "representation" may appear essentially as a "question" rather than as a "response").

12. In doing so, I have been influenced by Jacques Derrida's essay "*Geschlecht* I: Sexual Difference, Ontological Difference" (in *Psyche: Inventions of the Other,* vol. 2, eds. Peggy Kamuf and Elizabeth Rottenberg [Stanford: Stanford University Press, 2008]), in which Derrida links the "sexual neutralization" of Heideggerian *Dasein* to the "transcendental" gesture of establishing "ontological difference"— the object of existential analysis—*over and above* anthropological determinations.

13. In Jean-Claude Milner's recent work *L'Universel en éclats* (Lagrasse, France: Editions Verdier, 2014), where Milner opposes two "universals" (that is, in my terminology, two universalisms), he rightly accords fundamental importance to fact that the Latins (= Romans) converted what the classical Greeks (Aristotle) called *kath'holou* (literally, "according to the whole," hence "catholicity") into *universus/universum* (literally, "turned into one"). These are obviously two ways of thinking the "world" and inscribing difference within it that are not unrelated to the question that I am considering here. Similarly, although our definitions are not at all the same, it isn't entirely by chance that Milner identifies an "intense" universal and an extensive universal, as I have done in the past with equaliberty and the authority of the law. The fact remains that these binary antitheses are current throughout Western metaphysics.

14. In *The Theory of Moral Sentiments* (1759), the anthropological counterpoint to *The Wealth of Nations*, Adam Smith translates Cicero's *convenientia* as "propriety" (the etymological twin of "property"), which encapsulates the alternative *proper/improper*.

15. Translator's note: the pun on the French homophones "egos" and "égaux" (equals) is unfortunately partially lost in translation.

16. See G. Spivak, *A Critique of Postcolonial Reason* (Cambridge, Mass.: Harvard University Press, 1999); Max Marcuzzi's preface to his translation of Kant, *Géographie* (with Michèle Cohen-Halimi and Valérie Seroussi) (Paris: Aubier, 1999); and Raphaël Lagier, *Les Races humaines selon Kant* (Paris: Presses Universitaires de France, 2004). In his book *Kant in the Land of Extraterrestrials: Cosmopolitical Philosofictions* (trans. Will Bishop [New York: Fordham University

Press, 2013]), Peter Szendy shows that Kant, confronted with the question of the "character of the species," reaches the limit of the comparative method that had permitted him to assign *internal frontiers* to the human species by way of observable "characteristics." A "point of view" external to the species would thus be necessary. Yet one could also argue that the pragmatic equivalent of "nonhuman rational beings" (extraterrestrials) is represented, at the other end of the anthropological spectrum, by *those excluded from the inside,* those cut off from cultural progress by nature itself (the Fuegians, the Hottentots, the Aborigines), whose sudden emergence, as Spivak demonstrates, is symptomatic of the crucial moments at which "critique" is conceived as the faculty of judgment of humanity.

17. I describe this synecdoche, against which Frantz Fanon and Mary Wollstonecraft claim the universal in the name of women and blacks, in *Citizen Subject*, 280–86.

18. "Universalism of differences" (or cosmopolitism of differences) is Giacomo Marramao's expression, which he develops in the book *The Passage West: Philosophy after the Age of the Nation-State*, trans. Matteo Mandarini (London: Verso, 2012). Bloch uses the term "multiversum" in an essay from 1955, "Differentiations in the Concept of Progress" (in *A Philosophy of the Future* [New York: Herder and Herder, 1970]), where he challenges the "evolutionist" orthodoxy of GDR Marxism. The model that Bloch employs to theorize the intrinsic multiplicity of the "times" and "places" constitutive of history is a cosmological and above all musical model inspired by contemporary experiments in polytonality. See Remo Bodei, *Multiversum: Tempo e storia in Ernst Bloch* (Naples: Bibliopolis, 1982).

19. On the Humboldt brothers' work and the complementarity that unites them in a "cultural ecology" *avant la lettre*, see the papers presented at the symposium organized in 2014 at the Observatoire de Paris (as part of an exhibition of their work): "Les frères Humboldt: L'Europe de l'esprit." Also see Soraya Nour, "Le Cosmos et le cosmopolitisme d'Alexander von Humboldt," in *Le Soi et le cosmos d'Alexander von Humboldt à nos jours*, ed. Soraya Nour Sckell and Damien Ehrhardt (Berlin: Duncker and Humblot, 2015). John Leavitt, in *Linguistic Relativities: Language Diversity and Modern Thought* (Cambridge: Cambridge University Press, 2011), provides extensive commentary on the Humboldt brothers' thought, but it is to the late work of Franz Boas that he applies the term "multiverse." In all honesty, I should point out that, with regard to the differences in complexity of languages and, consequently, to their more or less "evolved" character, Wilhelm von Humboldt's position wasn't stable. Still, I think that egalitarianism is the logical tendency of his theory and distinguishes it from the Romantic proponents of the "superiority" of inflected languages (Indo-European) over "isolating" or "agglutinating" languages (Schlegel). Also see Jürgen Trabant, *Weltansichten: Wilhelm von Humboldts Sprachprojekt* (Munich: C.H. Beck, 2012).

20. See Balibar, *Citizen Subject*, Chapter 7 ("*Zur Sache Selbst*: The Common and the Universal in Hegel's *Phenomenology of Spirit*") and Chapter 2 above ("Constructions and Deconstructions of the Universal").

21. I have of course intentionally employed expressions characteristic of the thought of Hannah Arendt, who is the modern era's preeminent theorist of the realization of the community on the basis of this universalist requirement, in a movement that runs from the "decline of the nation-state" to the invention of new forms of political bonds.

22. *Acts of Citizenship*, ed. Engin Isin and Greg Nielsen (New York: Zed Books, 2008).

23. The reader will no doubt recognize here certain themes present in the work of Jacques Rancière and especially Jean-Luc Nancy, the latter of whom, on the heels of his exchange with Blanchot (1983) and in particular since *Being Singular Plural* (trans. Robert Richardson and Anne O'Byrne [Stanford: Stanford University Press, 2000]), has developed a far-reaching philosophy of being in common "without condition" (or without requisite identity, without the representation of a "common substance" of which individuals must partake in order to act or "co-appear" in the same world). In the process, however, Nancy has felt it necessary to theorize a "being with" that is no longer of the order of politics (which leads him to wonder if it might not be, as it was for Hegel, of the order of religion). If "plurality" is by definition constitutive of this "being with," it is highly doubtful that *anthropological differences* as such are part of the definition, unless they are elevated to the status of an ontological difference (which has a better chance of being the case for sexual difference than for cultural difference or for the difference between the normal and the pathological).

24. See his essay "Subjectivity in Language," in *Problems in General Linguistics*, trans. Mary Elizabeth Meek (Coral Gables, Florida: University of Miami Press, 1971).

25. Jean-François Lyotard, *The Differend: Phrases in Dispute*, trans. Georges Van den Abbeele (Minneapolis: University of Minnesota Press, 1989).

26. Jacques Derrida, "Abraham, the Other," in *Judeities: Questions for Jacques Derrida*, trans. Bettina Bergo and Michael B. Smith (New York: Fordham University Press, 2007), 15.

27. Étienne Balibar, *Droit de cité* (La Tour-d'Aigues: Editions de l'Aube, 1998). On the Saint-Bernard "sans-papiers" movement, see Madjigène Cissé, *Paroles de sans-papiers* (Paris: La Dispute, 1999), and the related articles, especially those by Alain Morice, published in *Plein Droit*, the journal of the Groupe d'information et de soutien des immigrés (GISTI).

28. Stefan Nowotny, "The Multiple Faces of the 'Civis.' Is Citizenship Translatable?" *Transversal* (April 2008), http://eipcp.net/transversal/0608/nowotny/en.

29. Émile Benveniste, "Deux modèles linguistiques de la cité," in *Problèmes de linguistique générale*, vol. 2 (Paris: Gallimard, 1974), 272–80.

30. Or, more precisely, to his alias, Valentin N. Voloshinov, author of *Marxism and the Philosophy of Language* (1930), whose attribution to Bakhtin is still disputed today.

31. To complicate matters still further, however, we should note that within the practice of collective action, the "sans papiers" are those who have (more or less completely) two or several languages at their disposal and can use them in order to establish positions of power, whereas their European counterparts, members of NGOs who rallied to their side for numerous actions (sometimes including hunger strikes), are confined to a single language or must resort to interpreters. Emmanuel Terray addresses this "reversal of fortune" with humor and insight in his essay "Le Troisième Collectif. L'Internationale des sans-papiers?" in *Plein Droit* 95, no. 4 (2012): 32–36.

32. In this regard, Nowotny's arguments follow very much the same lines as those of Gayatri Spivak, who has for many years looked at that other situation of "interrupted reciprocity," transcription: Western ethnologists' and colonial administrators' transcription of the discourse of their "native informants," which seems a remarkably perverse way of silencing the other by "giving them a voice" (or by *lending* them a voice in predetermined conditions). This is where she derives her idea (and practice) of a politics of translation that reverses, as much as possible (and via the essential pathway of literature), the hierarchy of "translated" and "translating" languages (see her collection of essays in *An Aesthetic Education in the Era of Globalization* [Cambridge, Mass.: Harvard University Press, 2012]).

33. On this point, see especially Emily Apter, *The Translation Zone* (Princeton: Princeton University Press, 2005).

34. The hypotheses at work in this final section were in part inspired by my reading of Lucie Mercier's doctoral dissertation, defended in 2015 at Kingston University London, entitled *The Inside Passage: Translation as Method and Relation in Serres and Benjamin*.

35. See Jacques Derrida, *The Monolingualism of the Other*, trans. Patrick Mensah (Stanford: Stanford University Press, 1998).

36. See her general introduction to the *Dictionary of Untranslatables*, ed. Barbara Cassin, translation eds. Emily Apter, Jacques Lezra, and Michael Wood (Princeton: Princeton University Press, 2014), as well as the collection of essays from the Cerisy conference: *Les Pluriels de Barbara Cassin*, ed. Philippe Büttgen, Michèle Gendreau-Massaloux, and Xavier North (Bordeaux: Éditions Le Bord de l'eau, 2014).

37. Note that neither French nor English are able to conserve exactly the near tautology of the German, because *Sprache* is normally translated as *langue* or

"language," while the verb *sprechen* becomes *parler* or "to speak" (referring to *parole* and *speech*, respectively).

38. Martin Heidegger, "Die Sprache" (1950), in *Unterwegs zur Sprache* (in English, "Language," in *Poetry, Language, Thought*, trans. Albert Hofstadter [New York: Perennial Classics, 2001]): "This is why we ask, 'In what way does language [speech] occur as language [speech] [*wie west die Sprache als Sprache*]?' We answer: *Language speaks* [*die Sprache spricht*]. [. . .] To reflect on language [speech] thus demands that we enter into the speaking of language [speech] [*auf das Sprechen der Sprache*] in order to take up our stay with language, i.e., within *its* speaking, not within our own. [. . .] We leave the speaking to language [speech]. We do not wish to ground language [speech] in something else that is not language itself, nor do we wish to explain other things by means of language [speech]" (188–89).

Étienne Balibar is Professor Emeritus of Moral and Political Philosophy at Université de Paris X–Nanterre; Distinguished Professor of Humanities at the University of California, Irvine; and Visiting Professor of French at Columbia University. His many books in English include *Citizen Subject: Foundations for Philosophical Anthropology* (Fordham, 2016), *Violence and Civility: On the Limits of Political Philosophy* (Columbia, 2016); *Equaliberty: Political Essays* (Duke, 2014); *We, the People of Europe? Reflections on Transnational Citizenship* (Princeton, 2003); *Politics and the Other Scene* (Verso, 2002); *Masses, Classes, Ideas: Studies on Politics and Philosophy before and after Marx* (Routledge, 1994), and two important co-authored books, *Race, Nation, Class: Ambiguous Identities* (with Immanuel Wallerstein; Verso, 1988) and *Reading Capital: The Complete Edition* (with Louis Althusser and others; Verso, 2016).

Joshua David Jordan translates twentieth- and twenty-first-century prose and poetry from the French. A specialist in the work of Henri Michaux, he teaches French literature and language at Fordham University. In 2015, he received a French Voices Award for his translation of David Lapoujade's *Aberrant Movements: The Philosophy of Gilles Deleuze.*

Roberto Esposito, *Terms of the Political: Community, Immunity, Biopolitics.* Translated by Rhiannon Noel Welch. Introduction by Vanessa Lemm.

Maurizio Ferraris, *Documentality: Why It Is Necessary to Leave Traces.* Translated by Richard Davies.

Dimitris Vardoulakis, *Sovereignty and Its Other: Toward the Dejustification of Violence.*

Anne Emmanuelle Berger, *The Queer Turn in Feminism: Identities, Sexualities, and the Theater of Gender.* Translated by Catherine Porter.

James D. Lilley, *Common Things: Romance and the Aesthetics of Belonging in Atlantic Modernity.*

Jean-Luc Nancy, *Identity: Fragments, Frankness.* Translated by François Raffoul.

Miguel Vatter, *Between Form and Event: Machiavelli's Theory of Political Freedom.*

Miguel Vatter, *The Republic of the Living: Biopolitics and the Critique of Civil Society.*

Maurizio Ferraris, *Where Are You? An Ontology of the Cell Phone.* Translated by Sarah De Sanctis.

Irving Goh, *The Reject: Community, Politics, and Religion after the Subject.*

Kevin Attell, *Giorgio Agamben: Beyond the Threshold of Deconstruction.*

J. Hillis Miller, *Communities in Fiction*.

Remo Bodei, *The Life of Things, the Love of Things*. Translated by Murtha Baca.

Gabriela Basterra, *The Subject of Freedom: Kant, Levinas*.

Roberto Esposito, *Categories of the Impolitical*. Translated by Connal Parsley.

Roberto Esposito, *Two: The Machine of Political Theology and the Place of Thought*. Translated by Zakiya Hanafi.

Akiba Lerner, *Redemptive Hope: From the Age of Enlightenment to the Age of Obama*.

Adriana Cavarero and Angelo Scola, *Thou Shalt Not Kill: A Political and Theological Dialogue*. Translated by Margaret Adams Groesbeck and Adam Sitze.

Massimo Cacciari, *Europe and Empire: On the Political Forms of Globalization*. Edited by Alessandro Carrera, Translated by Massimo Verdicchio.

Emanuele Coccia, *Sensible Life: A Micro-ontology of the Image*. Translated by Scott Stuart, Introduction by Kevin Attell.

Timothy C. Campbell, *The Techne of Giving: Cinema and the Generous Forms of Life*.

Étienne Balibar, *Citizen Subject: Foundations for Philosophical Anthropology*. Translated by Steven Miller, Foreword by Emily Apter.

Ashon T. Crawley, *Blackpentecostal Breath: The Aesthetics of Possibility*.

Terrion L. Williamson, *Scandalize My Name: Black Feminist Practice and the Making of Black Social Life*.

Jean-Luc Nancy, *The Disavowed Community*. Translated by Philip Armstrong.

Roberto Esposito, *The Origin of the Political: Hannah Arendt or Simone Weil?* Translated by Vincenzo Binetti and Gareth Williams.

Dimitris Vardoulakis, *Stasis before the State: Nine Theses on Agonistic Democracy*.

Nicholas Heron, *Liturgical Power: Between Economic and Political Theology*.

Emanuele Coccia, *Goods: Advertising, Urban Space, and the Moral Law of the Image*. Translated by Marissa Gemma.

James Edward Ford III, *Thinking Through Crisis: Depression-Era Black Literature, Theory, and Politics*.

Carlo Diano, *Form and Event: Principles for an Interpretation of the Greek World*. Translated by Timothy C. Campbell, and Lia Turtas; Introduction by Jacques Lezra.

Étienne Balibar, *On Universals: Constructing and Deconstructing Community*. Translated by Joshua David Jordan.

CPSIA information can be obtained
at www.ICGtesting.com
Printed in the USA
JSHW031443160720
6679JS00012B/2